GURU NANAK'S
TRAVEL TO HIMALAYAN
AND
EAST ASIA REGION

A NEW LIGHT

COL. D.S. GREWAL

NBS

NATIONAL BOOK SHOP
Pleasure Garden Market, Chandni Chowk, Delhi-110006

1995

ISBN 81-7116-177-4

Rs. 150

Published by
National Book Shop
Pleasure Garden Market,
Chandni Chowk, Delhi-110006

Typeset at
Singh Brothers
Bhogal, New Delhi

Printed at
Avon Offset Printers
Kuchan Chelan, Gali Rajan,
Darya Ganj, New Delhi

Contents

1 VARYING VISUALISATIONS OF GURUNANAK 2

BY SOBHA SINGH ARTIST

BY SIKKIMESE LAMAS

DIFFERENT VISUALISATIONS OF GURU NANAK

3

4

GOMPHAS / MONASTRIES VISITED BY GURU NANAK

5

6

7

THANGGU GOMPHA SIKKIM

8

PHODONG MONASTRY (SIKKIM)

9

RUMTEK MONASTRY (SIKKIM)

10

TAWANG MONASTRY COMPLEX (ARU)

11

SAKYA MONASTRY (TIBET)

12

SAMYA MONASTRY (TIBET)

13

LUMPUNG MONASTRY (ARU)

14

CELEBERATION AT HEMUS GOMPHA (LEH) PLACE CONTAINING IDOL OF GURU NANAK

15

ROUTE THANGGU TO GURU DONGMAR

16

THANG GU CHHORTEN

GURDWARA MANIKARAN SAHIB (ARU)

GURDWAR GURUDONGMAR (SIKKIM)

19

GURDWARA CHUNGTHANG

20

LAMA SAHIB PAD CHINH

21

22

PATHAR SAHIB CHUNGTHANG

23

GURDWARA GURU NANAK TAPASTHAN
MENCHUKA (ARU)

24

PATHAR SAHIB NIMU (LEH)

25

SCENE OF NANAK HILL NIMU LEH

26

CELEBERATIONS AT TAWANG GOMPHA

27

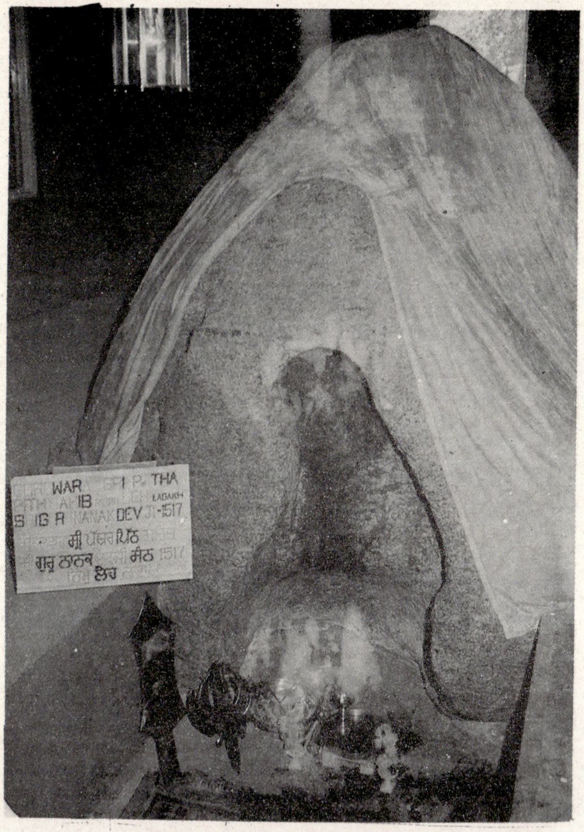

PATHAR SAHIB (LEH)

RING-DZINRIMPOCHE

DANACES PERFORMED IN MONASTRIES TO COMMEMORATE GURU NANAK'S VISIT

LAMAS PERFORMING DEVIL OANCE

LAMAS CELEBERATING GURU NANAKS VISIT TO MENCHUKHAVALLEY

31

AUTHOR AND PUBLISHER WITH THE PRESIDENT LATE GIANI ZAIL SINGH

32

AUTHOR PUBLISHER AND WRITERS AT RASHTRAPATI BHAWAN WITH THE PRESIDENT

Messages

1

It has given me a great pleasure to go through Colonel Grewal's book titled "Guru Nanak's Travels to Himalayan & East Asian Region—A New Light". The author has been working in this region in his capacity as an officer from the Government of India and has kept himself very well informed about the culture and traditions of the people of the region. Being a devout Sikh, he has been tracing the footprints of Guru Nanak Dev, the founder of his faith, who had been travelling extensively in this mountaneous area during his missionary tours for the spiritual elevation of the people of the region. The researches of Colonel Grewal regarding the Guru's itinerary in Sikkim, Bhutan and Tibet are noteworthy and interesting. He has consulted the available literature and has added his personal experience and information, wherever possible.

I appreciate the zeal with which the scholar is working regarding the travels of the Great Guru and am confident that he would be contributing a great deal with further researches on the subject. May the Guru enlighten him still more on the subject most dear to him and give him strength to continue his services as regards his literary endeavours.

sd/- xxx

Surindar Singh Kohli

Dr. Harnam Singh Shan
M.A. (Eng & Pbi) Ph.D.(London)
Honours in Persian and in Punjabi (Lahore)
R.R.A.S. (London), M.S.A. (Paris),M.B.S.(Edin.)

My dear Colonel Grewal ji,

Your research on 'Guru Nanak's travels to Himalayan Region' is of tremendous value. The extremely dedicated and devoted effort to find out something which is entirely new in Sikh history deserves not only appreciation but many many thanks, not only from me but from the entire society. I can only pray to God to keep you healthy, true-spirited and to be always fit and active in giving solid, productive and regular service to the community, society and culture, not only of our own people but of the entire world.

Dr. Harnam Singh Shan

15 Feb'93

Dear Col. Grewal,

"The Sikh Review" had been privileged, for many years during the late Capt. Bhag Singh ji's tenure as editor, to publish your fascinating travelogues that traced the Great Guru's journeys in India & beyond. Those narratives were a fascinating amalgam of history, traditions and theology of Sikhism, avidly read by the members of the Sikh Review family here & abroad.

I wonder if you still write on these journeys. We shall be happy to feature them.

With all good wishes.

Your's Sincerely
Saran Singh

About the Author

Dr. (Colonel) Dalvindar Singh Grewal is a senior officer of the Indian Army and is presently commanding an Artillery Regiment. Despite his heavy official commitments, his attachment to pen has been consistent and dedicated. He has been published and acknowledged widely in English, Punjabi and Hindi periodicals and has number of books to his credit. He has written about 250 entries for Punjab Kosh (Encyclopedea Punjab) prepared by Punjab Govt. He has also contributed for Shabad Jor Kosh, published by Punjabi University. He has given series of talks on All India Radio and appears occasionally on TV. He is a member, Board of Studies 'Weapon Systems' Poona University, and a reviewing member 'Encyclopedia Punjab'.

Birth. 04 April 1945,
Chak No 89 JB (Rattan), Layallpur. (now in Pakistan).
Father - S. Anokh Singh Grewal
Mother - Late Smt. Chand Kaur.
Qualifications.
M.A., M.B.A., L.L.B., Ph.D.,
A.M.I.B.M., P.G.D.T.E. (C.I.E.F.L.)
A.C.B.M. (Military College of E.M.E.)

Punjabi Books

Safar Sanjogi (Travelogue), Chingan (Poetry), Van-Suvane (General Essays), Chakarvyuh (Stories),
Sikh Shahidi Lehran (Sikh History), Merian Dharmik Yatravan (Travelogue) and Harimandir ton Rammandir (travelogue for children) (under print).

English Books

Aka, Miri-Aka and Miji Languages of Arunachal Pradesh : A Comparative Study, 'Culture and Kinship among Akas, Miri-Akas and Mijis of Arunachal Predesh', 'Culture and Languages of Tribes of Arunachal Preadesh', 'Membas of Arunachal', 'Amazing Journey of Guru Nanak to Himalayas' and 'Selected Essays', all under print.

Introduction

Guru Nanak, the founder of Sikhism, was born in an epoch making-period, the period of adventure, discovery, inquiry and renaissance. The adventures and discoveries not only led to physical achievements but also to colonalisation, domination, oppression and invasion, while the inquiry and renaissance led to the search into human existance and reformation in the oppressive systems.

The famous oppressors, invaders, traders and travellers like Bahlol Lodhi (1451-1489), Sikander Lodhi (1486-1517), Ibrahim Lodhi (1517-1526), Babur (1483-1530), Columbus (discovered America in 1492) and Vasco-da-Gama(discovered sea route to India in 1498), co-existed alongwith eminent reformists, sages and saints like Guru Nanak (1469-1538), Vallabhacharya (1479-1530), Chaitnya Mahaprabhu (1486-1533), Kabir (1440-1518), Namdev (1217-1351), Shankardev (1490-1637), Mira Bai (1499-1570), Eknath (1528-1595/1609), Dadoo (1544-1603), Tuka Ram (1608-1648), Isasmus (1466-1536), Zawang (1484-1531), Calvin (1564-1605) and Saint Francis Xavier (1506-52).

The political, cultural and religious situations were both disturbing and balancing. The political turmoil was countered by religious renaissance. The state of the political turmoil has been well described by Guru Nanak himself:-

"This age is like a dragon sword
The Kings are butchers,
Goodness has taken wings and flown".[1]

He adds:-

"There is no one who receiveth or giveth
not bribes.
The king administers justice only
when his palm has been greased (filled).[2]

The gloriously rich tradition of religious tolerance was powerless against the tyranny of the epoch, of the extreme bigotism. Dissent was carried to a point of intolerance and intolerance to unrivalled persecution. The warriors had conflicting desires to conquer and achieve wordly gains. They came, not as conquerors, but enemies and the face of Indian history was marred, if not charred, with these suppressive forces; for it was not the policies but the institutions which were ruthlessly oppressed. The invaders had trampled the rich civilisation of agesunder their feet, without the slightest remorse or inequity.

In an era of contention and confusion and in the background of these disabilities, the epoch of transition and interregnum in a suffering country, only a spiritual revolution could survive.

Backdrop to these historical developments in India, in which Guru Nanak chose his path are hence of consequence. From the tenth century onwards, successive hordes of invaders had poured in from Central Asia. As the highway to Delhi lay through the Punjab, the greatest suffering had been caused to the people of this province.

Bhai Gurdas (1531-1639 A.D.) described this situation in Guru Nanak's biographical accounts:-

> "Degeneration occured in the world, leading to the four-caste division and enactments about four stages of life. The sanyasis into ten, and the Yogis into twelve sects were divided. Various orders of hermits, Jain monks and unclad recluses set up endless recrimination debate. None practised the way of release from transmigration"

In this situation, in the words of the poet," Melting at the wail of humanity, The Lord sent Guru Nanak to earth"[3] to bring peace and reconciliation the first words that came from him on emerging from the rivulet Bein when the call came to him and he shouted, "There is no Hindu, no Musalman", thus presenting to mankind the image only of undivided humanity, wherein all men are brothers, without the walls created by warring creeds. Then in his passion to fulfill the divine mission entrused to him, Guru Nanak travelled far and wide. Everywhere his message was to seek the core of each faith, behind rituals and conventional appearances the essence of God-conciousness, the way to a noble life and the brotherhood of man.

The field of Guru Nanak's activity has been described by Bhai

Gurdas in his first '*var*' (verse), as 'the four lands and nine regions' to convey his message. Dr. Kohli quoting *Purans* mentions these regions to be Bharata, Kimpursha, Hari, Ilavarta or Krauncha, Ramyaka, Haranamaya or Hiranyaka, Kuru or Uttara Khand is the central region of Jambu Dwipa and is flanked by Bhadrasva Khand to the right and Ketumala Khand on the left. The uppermost region is Uttra-Khand and lowest Bharat Khand. Hiranamaya Khand and Ramayaka Khand lie between Bharat Khand and Illavrata. The seven Kulaparvata (Mountain ranges), in Jambu Dweep are Nila, Shweta, Hemkunt, Hamasna, Sringevena, Nishide and Sumeru. Guru Nanak is supposed to have visited these ranges also.[4] As per 'Janamsakhi Bhai Balla', 'Nanak Prakash of Bhai Santokh Singh' and 'Guru Nanak Suryoudai of Mahant Ganesha Singh', Guru Nanak visited following seven Dwipas; Jambu, Plaksha, Kusha, Salmali, Krauncha, Shaka and Pushkara[5].These dwipas have been identified by scholars as follows:-

	Col Gerini	*Wilford*	*Iyer*	*others*
Jambu	India	India	India	Major part of Asia
Plaksha	Arakan and Burma	Asia Minor	Greece	Basin of Mediterranian
Kusha	Sunda Archipelago	Iran	Iran, Saudi-Arabia and Ethopia	Iran and Iraq
Salmali	Malaya Peninsula	Central Europe	Sarmatia	Tropical part of Africa
Krauncha	South India	Western Europe	Asia Minor	Basin of Black Sea
Shaka	Kamboj	British	Scythia	Contries to South of Jambu Dwipa
Pushkara	North China and Malaysia	Iceland	Turkistan	Japan, Manchuria, and South-Eastern Siberia

No two researchers bring out the same results. However, generally the distribution shows the area coverage to be nearly the whole world except North and South America, Australia, Arctic and Antarctic regions.

This shows the vast coverage by Guru Nanak. It would have been nearly impossible in the days of tardy means of communications and their near non-availability to a common man. In Janamasakhi Bhai Balla this difficulty has been covered by giving an explanation that Guru flew through space, etc. While on Mount Una, he shuts his eyes. His disciples Bala and Mardana also shut their eyes. And when the eyes are opened on the instructions of the Guru, they find themselves on Mount Abu'. Possibly this explanation has been a copy of the myth about Pandavas who are described to have been flown into space from Mount Sumeru.

I have visited most of the places in Himalayas connected with Guru Nanak.From the information available, it clearly appears that:-

(a) He moved generally from one religious centre to another, visiting the centre of power also in the respective areas.

(b) He generally travelled on 'Yogi trails' sequentially.

(c) In mountains he travelled on foot from one place to another leaving no gaps to vouch for the myth according to which he could have covered the distance by flying. The myth, hence, does not hold ground.

The theory that he flew can be discarded in view of this. The other means by which he used to travel specially to foreign countries by sea of which sufficient information is available.

There are some names of the areas/states given in the Janamsakhis connected with his journey which had to be interpreted by the writer. The interpretations of the recorded local names or mixed-up names are given as follows:-

Names	*Present Equivalent*
Asa	Assam
Gujri	Gujrat
Tilang	Telengana
Dhanasari	Tenasserim in Burma/Area Around Dhanasari Rivers in Assam.
Sorath	Saurashtra
Kavru	Kamrup in Assam
Maru	Marwar
Habash	Abysinia and Sudan

Munafik	South Russia, North-West Kashmir and North-West Afghanistan
Bishambar	Bihar (around Patna)
Haru	Palitana and Mount Abu Area of Rajasthan/Gujrat
Singladip	Sri Lanka
Bhutant	Bhutan
Bisiar	Bushaar in Kumaon-Garhwal and Himachal Pradesh
Room	Turkey
Sham	Syria
Shvarnpur	Thailand

Guru Nanak having attained enlightenment, thought of redeeming the lost souls and putting them into a right path through God's name, "I left my home in search of the righteous and followed this course to evolve a new philosophy of life. Being a pedlar of truth, I am out to trade in truth. It is through the righteous that I shall ferry my followings accross the ocean of existance". (Ram Kali/SGGS, p.39)

Guru Nank started his journey to redeem the world with God's name, when he was in his twenties. He went to God's service through the service of mankind becoming Lords' bard. He travelled from Russia to Sri Lanka (North to South) and from China to Africa (East to West) for a period of about twenty-six years from 1498 to 1524. His travels are called as Udasis and said to be four in number, i.e.,

Udasi	Period	Places	Main Purpose
First	1498-1508	up to East Bengal	Hindu, Jain and Budhist centres.
Second	1508-1513	South: up to Sri Lanka	-do-
Third	1513-1518	North: up to Tibet & China.	Sidhas, Lamas & Budhist Centres.
Fourth	1518-1524	West: up to Arab & Africa	Islamic & Christianity Centres.

In his third Udasi from 1513 to 1518, he started from Kartarpur and visited the states of Himachal Pradesh,Uttrakhand (Garhwal & Kumoan Hills), Nepal, Tibet, Sikkim, Assam, Arunachal, Nagaland, Manipur, Tripura, Meghalaya, Bangladesh, Burma, Malaysia, China, Tibet, Kashmir & reached back in Punjab in 1518 A.D.

Third Udasi is explored the least by the researchers, possibly due to the difficulty of terrain and poor communication system in the areas. Information available is also scanty and full of myth. Guru Nanak was also known by different names e.g. Nanak Rishi, Nanak Lama, Guru Rimpoche etc, making his identity difficult.Hence identification of his visits could not be rightly established.

This reseacher collected whatever evidence was available and visited almost every place in the Himalayas to collect evidence. Evidence was available in the form of legends, names of places, material items and the traditions of worshipping of his idols and visits by lamas to Harmandir Sahib. The evidence was checked with the legends recorded in Janamsakhis and it turned out to be a logical and connected account. This account is given out here for the readers and the researchers, who I am sure, would not only gain some more information about Guru Nanak's amazing journey but will also go into details to explore further.

I must thank Smt.Amrita Pritam, late Capt. Bhag Singh, Dr. Surinder Singh Kohli, Late Dr. Tarlochan Singh, Dr. Harnam Singh Shan, S.Saran Singh ICS, Late Dr. Gurdial Singh Phul, S. Piara Singh Datta, Dr. Ajit Singh, S. Nirvair Singh Arshi and S. Jaswant Singh Ajit, who guided, inspired and encouraged me to continue with my research.Late Dr. Ganda Singh's name however needs special mention as he initiated me into this research.

I am also grateful to Major Jasbir Singh Gill, Capt.(now Lt col) Bikkar Singh, Shri Kholi Extra Asst Commissioner Manchukha, D.C. and PRO Tawang and Bomdila Districts of Arunachal who helped me in collecting evidence and to Dr.Boot of Centre for Himalayan Studies for preparing the maps.

I also thank my publishers National Book Shop, who not only encouraged me but also agreed to publish the work even when it was at the infant stage.

Nashik

Dalvinder Singh Grewal

References

1. Selections from the Sacred Writings of the Sikhs, P-82
2. Metcalffe, C., *The Sikh Religion*, Vol I, P-5).
3. Gurbachan Singh Talib, *Guru Nanak :* 1984, P.18-19.
4. Kohli S.S. (Dr.) 1969 (1978R), *Travels of Guru Nanak*. Chandigarh, Punjab University, P. 173-74.
5. Ibid, P.80.

Beginning of Sumer Udasi

Guru Nanak's third itinerary to Himalayan Region is known as Sumer Udasi. This is also known as 'his travels to Kailash-Mansarover'. Earliest accounts of this journey are found recorded in *'Varan-Bhai Gurdas'* in brief. Bhai Gurdas (1551-1639) writes:-

"Baba (Nanak) viewed the utmost extremities of the nine regions of the earth. He then ascended (mount) Sumeru where a company of Sidhs came into view".[1] Sumer is the name of legendry mountain which in relation to this journey has been identified as Mount Kailash.

All the Janamsakhis have the record of Guru Nanak's visit not only to Mount Kailash/Sumer, but also to the adjoining areas. Maximum details about this journey are in Janamsakhi Bhai Bala. In *Walait Wali Sakhi,* this journey is recorded under '*Uttar Khand ki Udasi*' also stated as Third Udasi. The dress worn by Guru Nanak in this Udasi is stated to be as follows, "Skin in feet (animal skin shoes) and on head (animal skin head cover), complete body covered and 'tikka' (paste) of 'kesar' (vermillion) on forehead[2]. In this Udasi his food was of flowers and fruits of wild plant (akk)"[3].

Accompanying him were Hassu Lohar (Blacksmith) and Sihan Chhinba (Tailor)[4].

Janamsakhi Meharban by Sodhi Meharban (1581-1640) gives the start, point of this Udasi as Sultanpur, 'after the discussions at Gorakh Hatri[5]. Janamsakhi Bhai Balla (stated to have been written by Guru Angad on the dictation of Bhai Balla) does not give dress or food habits of Guru Nanak but states Balla and Mardana as his companions. He gives the charonology of this Udasi to be after his visit to the West. All other Janamaskhis describe this visit before his visit to the West. Beginning of this Udasi is given from Sultanpur. The places visited are given as Himachal, Sumer, Munufik Des and various mountains e.g. Hem, Sirdhar, Una, Koona, Meena, Seela, Eena, Ikhan, Girnar and Ulak and sea ports of Ghurat Bander, Lahndi Bander, Machhli Bander, Laisal

Khand, Sri Lanka, Darbala city, Khuram (Khurrum) and Setbandu-Rameshwaram. There are also records of his visits to Asrapan, Chittagong, Bisihar island, Brahampur, Plaksha-dweep, Silmila Dweep, Suwaranpur, Deogandhar and Parsar Nama, before going to Sumer[7].

Janamsakhi B-40 (ed Piar Singh) gives details of Guru's visit to Triya Des (Kamrup) (p85-6), Sumer (p86-91), Bhutan (p124-5), Kashmir (p125-6) and Himachal (p139-40) in that order. Bala and Mardana are stated to be his companions. This travel is shown after his visit to Mecca[8].

Janamsakhi, by Bhai Mani Singh, a contemporary of Guru Gobind Singh, mentions that (after Sri Lanka) Guru visited Kush Dweep and Pushkar Dweep after leaving Jambu Dweep and visited Sumer thereafter. He also visited Meena Parbat. From Sumer, Guru Nanak is stated to have gone to Jammu. Kartarpur was established by him after Sumer Udasi, according to this Janamsakhi. His visit to the North and East Asia is also covered under this Udasi[9].

Though a bibliography has been given out at the end of the book, important sources in addition to the Janamsakhi's which give account ot Guru Nanak's Sumer Udasi are as follows:-

(a) Bhai Behlo's 'Suchak Prasang'. Bhai Behlo was a contemporary of Guru Arjan Dev and died on 24 March 1706.
(b) Baba Sarup Chand's 'Mahima Prakash' (Vartak).
(c) Parchian Sewa Das.
(d) Pracheen Panth Prakash by Rattan Singh Bhangu.
(e) Nanak Prakash, Twarikh Guru Khalsa and Gurdham Prakash by Giani Gyan Singh.
(f) Nanak Prakash by Bhai Santokh Singh.
(g) Guru Khalsa Twarikh by Giani Lal Singh-Sangrur.
(h) Jeevan Charit, Guru Nanak Dev ji by Dr. Trilochan Singh.
(i) Travels of Guru Nanak by Dr. Surinder Singh Kohli.
(j) Atlas of Travels of Guru Nanak by Drs. Fauja Singh and Kirpal Singh.

Bhai Behlo Mentions Guru Nanak's visit to Sidh Matta, Nanak Matta, Kavroo Des (Kamrup) and Keet Raj (Baij Nath) and of Guru meeting Madhur Bain, Devloot, Jhanda, Kamalnain etc, as well as Sidhas at Sumer. His material source appears to have been Janamsakhi Bhai Balla. Mahima Prakash (Vartak) of Baba Sarup Chand (1741) also mentions Sumer and Nanak Matta but no detailed accounts are given.

Next account is by Sewa Dass (Parchian Sewa Das). Guru Nanak's visit to Sumer Parbat, meeting 84 Sidhs (including Gorakh Nath) and reciting Japji and Sidh Goshat at Sumer are mentioned. This account too, appears to have been extracted from Janamsakhi Bhai Balla.

Rattan Singh Bhangu Shahid also touches (Pracheen Panth Prakash) upon Guru Nanak's travels to Himalayan Region in 'Pahile Mahale ki Sakhi' and mentions 'Rikhikesh, (Rishikesh), Gorakhmatta, Badri Nath and Kedar Nath as the places having been visited by Guru Nanak. He does not mention Sumer or Kailash.

The account of 'third itinerary' given by Giani Lal Singh Sangrur in *'Guru Khalsa Twarikh'* (first pub. in 1940) (p. 98-108) is more detailed and includes new places visited during this journey. These include Sultanpur, Kalanaur, Gurudaspur, Dasuha, Kotla, Trilokinath, Ghumeran, Kangra, Jwalaji Mandir, Rawalsar, Chamba, Kulu, Bijlian-Mahadev, Braham Koti, Manikaran, Doon Teerath, Kahloor, Kiratpur, Nalagarh, Handoor, Panjore, Dhara-Teerath, Mahisar, Dehradun, Masoori, Chadrata, Bushahar, Kashi, Goumukhi-Ganga, Kahkadwal, Srinagar (Garhwal), Badri Narayan, Bhimkot hills, Sumer, Ranikhet, Garh-Mukteshwar, Nainital, Gorakhmatta, Nanakmatta, Gorakhpur, Pauri, Kotdwar, Neemkhar, Ayudhia, Raniganj, Sitamarhi, Old Baksar, Kanchan-Ganga, Janakpur, Chatar Nagar, Bagkshetar Teerath, Dhomri, Shivpur, Brahamkund, Lakhanpur, Lalta-Patti, Tamlang, Aamlang, Tashi, Garu Kunbha, Askrode, Chumbhial Mountain Range, Tibet, Lake Mansarovar, Kailash, Yarkand, Ladakh, Bhotlasa, Jhankar-River-banks. Shorkot Lusak, Gilgit, Askardu, River Sheshnag, Lake Wooler in Sri Nagar, Bhadarwah, Panger Des, Manmeh, Kular, Dhaulidhar, Dalhouzi, Mankot, Trikaata, Vaishno Devi, Jammu, Parmandli Teerath, Chalaini, Jasrota, Madhopur, Sujanpur, Pathankot, Gurdaspur, Sultanpur and Talwandi. The period given is 15 Aug 1574, Bikrami to 17 Kartik Samrbat 1575 and place of origin of Udasi is Kartarpur[10].

In Panth Prakash (p.59-62) Giani Gyan Singh gives the names of places visited in Sumer Udasi (Uttar Khand Udasi) by Guru Nanak as follows:-

Kangra, Jawalamukhi, Kahloor, Kiratpur, Gorakhpur, Nanak-Matta, Gorakh-Matta, Nepal, Sikkim, Bhutan, Himalaya ranges, Man-Mahesh, Ahi-la-chen, Al-la-chen, Lhasa, China, Kashmir, Punger Dess, Vaishno Devi, (Kamroop) Kachhar, Assam, Manipur, and Bangla-(Bangla Desh) in first Udasi (p.49-51).

Later accounts i.e.by Bhai Santokh Singh (1883), Bhai Gian Singh and Bhai Veer Singh, though follow Janamsakhi Bhai Balla, yet they try to eliminate myth which affected the authenticity of earlier account.

Dr. Trilochan Singh (Jeevan Charit Guru Nanak Dev ji (1972) Dr. Surinder Singh Kholi, (Travels of Guru Nanak) and Dr. Fauja Singh and Kirpal Singh (Atlas of Guru Nanak's Travels) are the other important researchers who have recorded the account of Guru Nanak's travels to Himalayan region in some detail.

The later researchers give out the following routes to Sumer:-

(a) Punjab-Himachal Pradesh-Sumer-Kashmir-Punjab (Achal Vatala) (Atlas of Travels of Guru Nanak by Drs. Fauja Singh Kirpal Singh).

(b) Punjab-Himachal Pradesh-Uttarkhand-Kailash-Sumer-Nepal-Tibet-Sikkim-Bhutan and Kartarpur. Guru Nanak's Journey to Kashmir and Ladakh is given in different Udasis. (Dr. Trilochan Singh's Jeevan Charit-Guru Nanak Dev).

(c) Punjab-Himachal Predesh-Uttarkhand-Kailash (Sumer)-Mansarovar-North Eastern Uttar Pradesh-North Bihar-Nepal-Tibet-Sikkim-Bhutan-(Tarai Region)-China-Ladakh-Kashmir-Punjab. (Giani Lal Singh Sangrur in Guru Khalsa Twarikh & Dr. Surinder Singh Kohli in Travels of Guru Nanak).

If we analyse the available material, we find that:-

(a) The earliest detailed account of Sumer Udasi is available in Janamsakhi Bhai Balla. Almost all the later writers follow the version given by him, discarding the myth elements as far as possible. The fact behind the acceptance of Bhai Balla's Janamsakhi appears to be the prevalent belief that this Janamsakhi was written by Guru Angad (1539-52), Guru Nanak's Successor, from the dictation of Bhai Balla, reputed to be one of the First Guru's associate. This claim has however been rejected by various researchers, who give more authority to Puratan Janamsakhi and Janamsakhi Meharban.

(b) Earlier accounts of Sumer Udasi are not giving the correct period, places visited and the people met by Guru Nanak during this Udasi. The dress and the food habits of Guru Nanak are given only in Puratan Janamsakhi which, in the absence of any other account, have to be given due credit.

(c) Generally all the Janamsakhis agree that 'Guru Nanak visited Himalayan region after his first Udasi and before he went to Kamroop and East Asian Countries. Sumer Udasi is not found properly linked with Guru's journey to Kamroop & East Asia clearly, though the period of Sumer Udasi is also stated as 12 Years. In Janamsakhi Bhai Balla, it is mentioned that Guru Nanak visited Sumer after visiting all the islands (of East Asia).

This researcher had the privilege of visiting most of the Himalayan region and Assam and obtained some information from Burma, Tibet and China through sources and came to the conclusion that Guru Nanak's travels to Himalayan region covered portion of East Punjab-Himachal Pradesh-Garhwal-Kumaon Hills-Kailash-Mansarovar area-Tarai Region of Uttar Predesh-North Bihar-Nepal-Sikkim (Via Tibet)- Bhutan-Arunchal Pradesh- Assam- Nagaland - Burma- Manipur- Mizoram-Bangladesh- Malaya- Indonesia- Bali- Thailand- Laos- Vietnam- China-North Eastern Tibet- Ladakh- Kashmir and Northern Punjab. This route is more or less the same as discribed by Dr. Surinder Singh Kohli.

The Period of this Travel has been given differently by different researchers:-

(a) Giani Lal Singh Sangrur gives this period to be between *15 Asuj 1574 Bikrami to 17 Kartik 1575 Bikrami.* This Period according to English Calender is of 1517 A.D. to 1518 A.D.[11]

(b) Dr. Surinder Singh Kohli gives out this period to be from 1514 AD to 1517 A.D.[12]

(c) Giani Lal Singh gives this period to be from 1515 to 1517 A.D.[13].

(d) S. Sahib Singh gives the dates as Samvat 1573 to 1575 i.e. 1516 to 1518 A.D.[14].

Similarly other writers also differ about the total period. This is, probably due to the uncertainty which prevails over the distance and route covered and places visited.

Most of these writers include Guru's journey to East Asia in first itinerary where the total period given is about 12 years. They also do not include Tibet and China in this Udasi. In case Guru Nanak visited East in his Uttar or Sumer Udasi, the period taken has to be much more as is given in Janamasakhi Bhai Balla where the sea journey itself took even more than one month sometimes to each island and Guru stayed in the islands for months.

Janamsakhi states that Guru went to Sumer after visiting Silmila Dweep and Suwaran Dweep[15]. Giani Lal Singh Sangrur mentions that Guru Nanak went to China after Assam and Burma (Rangoon, Mandley), Dr. Surinder Singh Kohli States that it was about 1517 when Guru Nanak entered Provinces of China. He further states the route adopted by Guru Nanak from Nanking.

In view of this information, it can be tentatively presumed that Guru Nanak visited East Asian countries after his visit to Assam. The time of his visit attributed to these areas has to be included in this itinerary.The start of this journey will have to be around the year 1512 or 1513 and completion in the Year 1517 or 1518. To Sum up we can safely deduce that:-

(a) Guru Nanak completed his Sumer Udasi between 1512 to 1518 AD.

(b) He wore clothes made of skins, suitable for hills. His food was of wild plants.

(C) He had Bhai Balla, Mardana, Sihan Chhimba and Hassu Lohar as his campanions.

(d) He started from Sultanpur, visited Himachal Pradesh, Uttar Khand, Sumer, Terai Regions of Uttar Pradesh, North Bihar, Nepal, Sikkim, Bhutan, Arunachal pradesh, Assam, Nagaland, North-West-Burma, Manipur, Mizoram, Tripura, South East Bangladesh, Southern Burma, Malaya, Indonesia, Thailand, Laos, Vietnam, China, Tibet and Kashmir before reaching back in Punjab.

References

1. Ganda Singh (ed), Sources on the life and teachings of Guru Nanak, Guru Nanak's Birth Quincentenary Volume, *The Punjab Past and Present*, Vol III. Patiala, Punjabi University, 1969.

2. *Walait Wali Janamsakhi* (ed) Dr. Kirpal Singh, Patiala, Punjabi University, P. 49.
3. Ibid
4. Ibid
5. *Meherban Wali Janamsakhi* (ed) Dr. Kirpal Singh Patiala, Punjabi University, P. 140-1.
6. *Janamsakhi Bhai Balla,* Dr. Kirpal Singh Patiala, Punjabi University , P. 259.
7. ———————— Op.Cit P. 264-300.
8. *Janamsakhi* B-40 (ed) Piar Singh, Amritsar, Guru Nanak Dev University.
9. *Janamsakhi Bhai Mani Singh* (ed,) Dr. Kirpal Singh, Patiala, Punjabi University : P.253-5.
10. Lal Singh (Giani), *Guru Khalsa Twarikh,* Lahore Book Shop, Ludhiana, 1940 (3rd edn 1985), P. 99-108.
11. Lal Singh Sangrur (Giani), P. 108.
12. Surinder Singh Kohli (Dr.) P. 109 to 131.
13. *Punjabi Dunia,* Guru Nanak Number Part I 22 - No. 11 - 12, P. 35.
14. Sahib Singh, *Jeevan Birtant Guru Nanak Devji* - P.85.
15. *Janamsakhi Bhai Balla* (ed), Kirpal Singh, P. 280.
16. Lal Singh Sangrur (Giani), P. 71.
17. Surinder Singh Kohli (Dr.), P. 128.

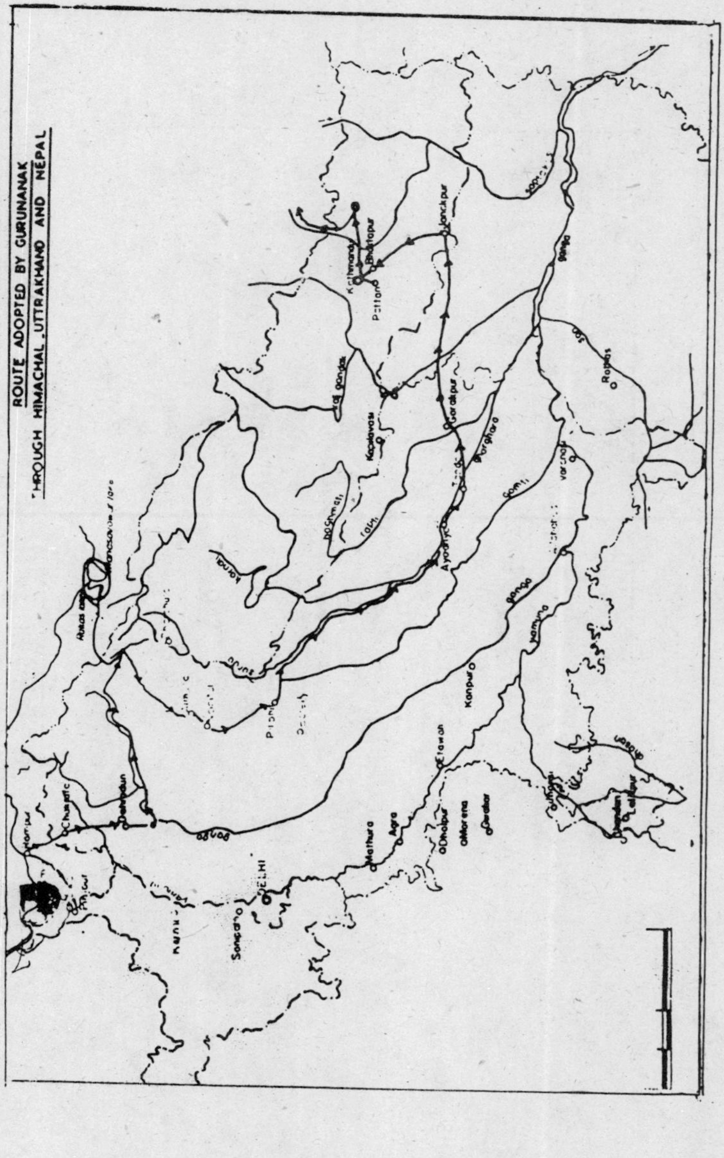
ROUTE ADOPTED BY GURUNANAK
THROUGH HIMACHAL, UTTRAKHAND AND NEPAL
DELHI
Mathura
Agra
Kanpur
Etawah
Ayodhya
Gorakhpur
Kapilavastu
Kathmandu
Pattan
Janakpur
Rohtas
Ganga
Yamuna
Gomti
Dehradun

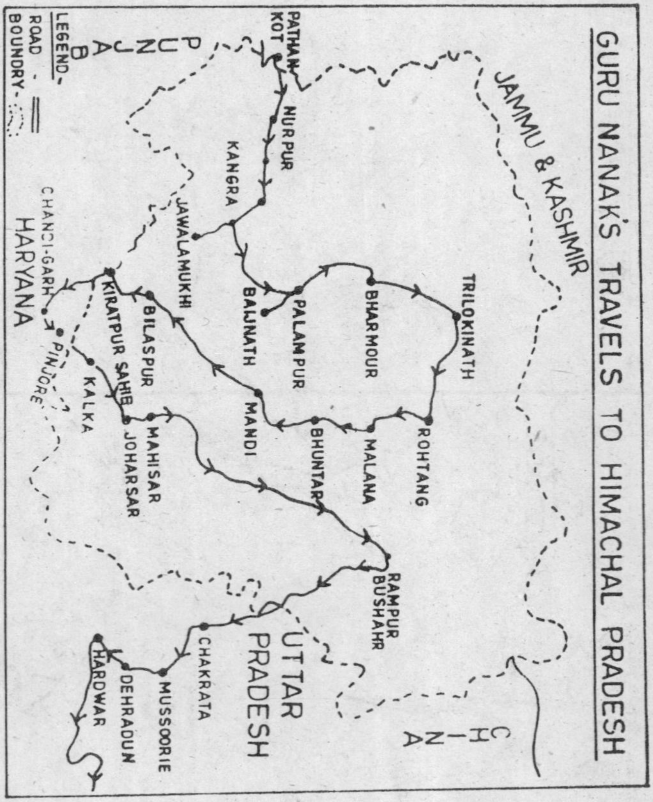
GURU NANAK'S TRAVELS TO HIMACHAL PRADESH
JAMMU & KASHMIR
CHINA
TRILOKINATH
BHARMOUR
ROHTANG
MALANA
BHUNTAR
PALAMPUR
BAIJNATH
MANDI
PATHANKOT
NURPUR
KANGRA
JAWALAMUKHI
BILASPUR
KIRATPUR SAHIB
MAHISAR
JOHARSAR
KALKA
PINJORE
CHANDI-GARH
HARYANA
PUNJAB
RAMPUR BUSHAHR
UTTAR PRADESH
CHAKRATA
MUSSOORIE
DEHRADUN
HARDWAR
LEGEND-
ROAD -
BOUNDRY -

Himachal Pradesh

Himachal Pradesh was a part of Punjab till 1966 when during reorganisation of Punjab on linguistic basis it was formed as a separate state. During Guru Nanak Dev's period it was divided in different princely states namely Chamba, Mandi, Suket, Sirmur, Bushahar and 20 other smaller states in the hills as well as the hilly areas of Punjab like Kangra, Simla, Lahaul and Spiti.

The area of the state is rugged and mountainous and is bounded by Tibet in the North-East, Kashmir in the North, Punjab in the West and Haryana and Uttar Predesh in the South-West and South respectively. The Eastern border is also common with the hills of Uttar Pradesh.

'The valleys of Kangra, Chamba, Kulu, Lahul and Spiti are the most exciting valleys full of flora, fauna and natural beauty'.[1] The temples of Himachal pradesh are as exciting for temple enthusiasts as its scenic beauty is for nature lovers. 'There are more than 6000 temples dotting the hills of Himachal, famous ones being Baijnath temple, Lakshmi-Narayan temple, Jwalaji, Hidamba Devi temple and Basheshar Mahadev temple'.[2] Also the Bodh temple at Rawalsar in the memory of Padamsambhawa is of great importance to Tibetan Lamas as this is their chief pilgrimage centre after Bodh Gaya and Kapilavastu.

In order to create order in the disorderly system and to find a way out from the tyranny of the rulers, Guru Nanak thought it fit and proper to bring the saints, sadhus, sidhs and yogis into mainstream to lead the people into the path of truth and enlighten them in darkness. His travels to various religious centres and centres of powers were conducted with this aim. Details of Guru Nanak's travels to Himachal are given out in various *Janam Sakhis*. In *Janam Sakhi Bhai Balla* (ed. Dr. Kirpal Singh p-286), the visit is stated as follows:-

'Then he flew off to Himachal and stood over Himachal Mardana enquired, 'Guruji, what place is this?' Guru stated, 'Mardana, this is Himachal'. Mardana said, 'This is whitish.' Guru Nanak then explained,

'Mardana, this is a white snow. In case a human being keeps feet in the snow, these get frozen; hence, this place in not worth living for human beings'. Mardana further enquired, 'Why did then, we come over here?' 'God has brought us,' replied Guru Nanak.

Mardana further asked, 'Is there any other place beyond this?' Guru Nanak answered, 'Mardana, Hem is ahead of this place'. 'Will you go there as well?', Mardana was anxious to know. Guru Nanak replied affirmatively. Therefrom they proceeded to Sirdhar Parbat'.

Guru Nanak visited Himachal Pradesh enroute to Sumer (Kailash) the key centre of Sidhs and also to other religious centres in Uttarkhand, it is likely that while at Rawalsar he came across various lamas and got attracted towards Tibetans and as a sequel to this he visited Tibet.

Guru Nanak after his first travel, on the request of Bhai Doda established Kartarpur and settled his family there. 'His later travels originated from Kartarpur itself'[4] 'Guru's third journey too started from Kartarpur wherefrom he crossed Ravi river on to Dera Baba Nanak, Kalanour and Gurdaspur'[5] and 'through Sujanpur and Pathankot entered Himachal pradesh'[6] and via Nurpur, and Kotla reached Ghumeran. 'At Ghumeran he blessed Arjan, a Tapa' wherefrom he proceeded to Kangra and held discourses with the pandits of Mahamaya Temple and explained them the true path.

Jwalamukhi

From Kangra, Guru Nanak visited the ancient temple of Goddess Jwalamukhi, another famous Hindu pilgrimage centre where a volcanic fire erupts nonstop from the earth, burns day and night and is said to be inflamed by the Goddess herself.[7] The temple of Jawalamukhi is considered as one of the fifty one Shaktipeeths. At Jwalamukhi he met Arjan Tapa again and held discussions with him. Near Gorkh Dibbhi, a Sikh temple commemorates the visits of the Guru.

Chamba area

'From Jawlamukhi, Guru Nanak went to Dharamsala and then to Chamba area and visited Bharmaur and Man Mahesh Lake'[8]. He proceeded to Trilokinath and Manikaran and returned through Dharamsala. 'From Dharamsala he went to Palampur and then to

Baijnath'[9]. Baijnath was known as Keedgram at that time. He visited the famous Baijnath temple and also on invitation of the local King had meals with him. Thereafter he proceeded to Manikaran. A Sikh temple and a spring commemorate Guru's visit to this place.

Mandi

'From Manikaran Guruji went to Mandi Suket where he forbade the ruler from idol-worship and directed him to get tuned to the One 'The God'[10].

Rawalsar

'Guru Nanak's next stay was at Rawalsar, a famous pilgrimage centre for Hindus and Buddhists[11]. He came in contact with Lamas at this place and explained them the true path of salvation. Besides, Lord Shankar and Lakshmi Narayan temples, Gurdwara Sahib commemorates Guru's visit. Later Guru Gobind Singh also paid his obeisance at the place and rested on a nearby hill for some time.

Kiratpur

'From Rawalsar Guru Nanak returned to Mandi and passed through Bilaspur district and reached Kiratpur (Punjab) where he met the Muslim divine named Buddhan Shas and bowed before his spiritual greatness'[12]. It is recorded that a tamed tiger used to control the goats of that saint. (Kiratpur Sahib is about 11 Kilometers from Anandpur Sahib towards Ropar.) Sayyad Buddhan Shah presented milk which the Guru did not drink, saying that he would drink it at another occassion. The faqir preserved the milk in a pot. According to a myth, later Baba Gurudita, the eldest son of sixth Guru appeared in the physical form of Guru Nanak on the instructions of Guru Hargobind and consumed it. Now a Gurdwara Sahib stands by the side of Bhakara Nangal canal close by the tomb of Sayyad Buddhan Shan.

Pinjore

'From Kiratpur, Guru Nanak proceeded to Pinjore (Now in Haryana). A fair of Akha Teej at Jag-Dhara was in Progress where a number of saints and sidhas had come. Guru Nanak had discourses with them and put them on right path [13]. A Gurdwara commemmorates Guru's visit to the place.

Joharsar

'Guru Nanak reached Joharsar Teerath (Near Dagshai) from Pinjore. A demon used to kill the calves of the area. Guru forced the demon out by his spiritual powers and eased the situation. The people there used to shave hair of their young children and kill animals for feasting sadhus'. 'Guru Nanak discouraged them from this practice and exhorted them to lead a virtuous life. People follow the instructions of Guru Nanak to this day. Gurdwara Joharsar commemmorates Guru's visit to the place.[14]

Mahisar

'From Joharsar Guru Nanak proceeded towards a place now called Mahisar (55 KMs from Subathu). Guru sat on the summit of a hill.The people of the nearby villages gathered around Guru Nanak and under the leadership of their saint Mahi requested him for water as there was no water around. He removed a stone with his stick. Lo! A spring gushed out. Mahi construced a tank for the storage of water. The water tank and the place since then are known as Mahisar[14]. The people of the place have their faith in Guru Nanak ever since and are his disciples.

'Guru Nanak proceeded to Rampur Bushahar through Shimla at Bushahar, Guru Nanak held discussions with the king and put him on the right path[15]. His journey further to Kailash-Mansarovar has two versions. According to one version he proceeded up North-East and reached Kailash along Satluj river. A temple in memory of Guru's visit near Puh is cited in support of this version. Naib Subedar Daljit Singh Head Priest of Gurdwara Sahib Artillery Centre Nashik Road told me of a place in Himachal Pradesh on the bank of Satluj river close to the Indo-Tibetan Border Pass Shipkila connected with Guru Nanak's visit to Sumer. He stated, "At a place 4 to 5 km from Puh close to the bank of Satluj near the Ship-kila Pass (2 hours journey & 5-6 km Distance), we visited Chela Mandir situated at a height. It is a Bodhi Temple whose priest was about 60 years old lama. The priest told us that ' the temple was erected in the memory of Guru Nanak's visit to the place. An idol of Guru Nanak of size 2x1/2 feet is etched on a stone in the temple. The ancestors of the lama had been celebrating the event of the visit of Guru to the place and the place has been regularly manned and worshipped ever since. Puh is about 2 days journey from Kalka (Chandigarh) wherefrom a bus service connects Puh through Shimla. Buses halt at Jhakhri near Bhaba Power Plant for the night. Shimla to Puh is about 14 hours journey. A Gurdwara has also been constructed at Puh by the Army but it is at a different location". The Subedar could not provide me the details about the time of visit to Guru Nanak and when the celebrations are held in the Bhudhist Temple. He was also not aware of the routes to Tibet from Puh.

According to second version from Rampur Bushahar, the Guru proceeded through, Chakrata, dehradun and Musoori and reached Hardwar. Places connected with Gurus visit on this route are cited, as the prrof of his visit on this route.

References

1. Gerner Manfred and Ahluwalia H.P.S. (Major) (1985) *Himalaya : A Practical Guide, Himalayan Books,* New Delhi. P. 192
2. Ibid, P. 193
3. Gian Singh Gyani-*Panth Prakash,* Language Department Punjab, Patiala, 1970, P-9.
4. Lal Singh Giani- *'Punjabi Dunia',* Language Department Punjab, Patiala, P. 38.
5. Kirpal Singh (Dr.) *Janam Sakhi Pramapara : Janam Sakhi Bhai Bala,* Punjabi University, Patiala 1969, P. 287.
6. Lal Singh Giani, *Guru Khalsa Twarikh,* Lahore Book Shop, Ludhiana, P. 99.
7. Ibid
8. Ibid
9. Kirpal Singh (Dr.) : *Janam Sakhi Prampra : (Janam Sakhi Bhai Mani Singh),* Punjabi University, Patiala, 1968, P.37.
10. Ibid P. 103
11. Lal Singh Giani, *Guru Khalsa Twarikh,* P. 99.
12. Kohli, Surinder Singh - *Travels of Guru Nanak,* Punjab University, Chandigarh P. 110.
13. Pandit Tara Hari Narotam , *Sri Guru Teerath Sangreh.* Temple Press, Ambala. (18-44), P-23.
14. Kohli, Surinder Singh. *Travels of Guru Nanak,* P. 111
15. Kirpal Singh (Dr.) *Janam Sakhi Prampra - Walaitwali Janam Sakhi,* P. 27

Garhwal-Kumaon Hills

'The hill regions of Uttar Pradesh, comprising of eight hill districts of Almora, Chamoli, Dehradun, Nainital, Pauri-Garhwal, Pithoragarh, Tehri Garhwal and UttarKashi has come to be known as Uttarkhand, This region is also popularly known as Garhwal and Kumaon Hills. Garhwal consists of Chamoli, Dehradun, Pauri and Tehri districts while Kumaon consists of Almora, Nainital and Pithoragarh districts. Uttarkhand is a conglomeration of shrines, temples, terraced-fields, meandering valleys with lush green meadows, yawning glaciers, glittering peaks and above all the selfless and friendly hill-folk. The exotic flora and fauna attract immensely and first and last impression of Uttarkhand on any visitor is that of peace and tranquility'[1].

It is this reason that sages made Uttarkhand their home and did meditation for years to attain salvation. The amount of meditation done on this land has earned it the name of Devbhumi, the dwelling place or abode of Gods. This is the very reason that people of Uttarkhand are so peace loving and have a deep rooted faith in God and in their religion. Every place in Uttarkhand, in one way or another, has its legend and folklore and religious link to the Puranic period. The area has numerous holy places and shrines such as Gangotri, Yamnotri, Badrinath, Kedarnath and Tapovan that dot Uttarkhand.

In Guru Nanak's time, various saints, sages, sidhas and yogis, had made this area as their abode to avoid the wrath of Slave Kings and the Mughals. Instead of facing and guiding the public on a true path they had found a recluse. This had created a lot of disenchantment in the general public as they were not finding any one to guide them in their times of distress. Guru Nanak took upon this journey to the hills not only to visit the saints, sidhas and yogis and to convince them to return to the general public and guide them but also to show them that salvation can be attained even in family life. This situation is very well explained by Bhai Gurdas in his verses.

'Sin has enslavened the world and (Dharma) the bull, standing beneath the earth cries (in anguish)
The sidhas sit silent in the mountains; who then will guide the world?
The yogis (who wander in the plains) are devoid of knowledge, Day and night thay plaster their limbs with ashes and do nothing'

(Bhai Gurdas: Waran: Var 1:25)

Baba (Nanak) visited the places of pilgrimage (tirath). He went round seeing them all (specially) on festival days. Many people were performing the rites of old religion. But being devoid of loving adoration these earned them no merit. God had not preordained them to practise love: (and so the Guru) found them reading the four Vedas and Smritis (instead)...... ..... *(Bhai Gurdas : Var 1: 25)*

Guru Nanak met ascetics devotees of rigorous virtue, defied mortals, yoga adept sidhs, nathas, gurus and disciples...........

(Bhai Gurdas: Var 1:26)

He visited almost all the important religious places of Uttarkhand in Sumer Udasi and met various sidhas, yogis, saints and ascetics and preached the path of Truth and by showing them the true path he guided them to lead the public in right direction in their hour of need, and take the world out of darkness of ignorance. From Rampur Bushahar in Himachal pradesh, Guru Nanak is stated to have proceeded through Chakrata, Dehradun and Massouri according to a version and reached Hardwar.

Hardwar

'At Hardwar, he proceeded to Harki Pauri. There, a crowd of pilgrim's led by priests was performing various rituals to obtain salvation for their dear departed ones.

He saw a multitude of the people offering water towards the sun with their right hands. He moved forward, stood facing the priests and began to offer water with his left hand towards the west. At this strange reaction attention of all others around was diverted towards Guru Nanak.

One of the priests moved forward and said, 'O ignorant one ! What are you doing? Come, I will help you to do what is right'.

"I am doing just what you were doing', replied the Guru and continued offering water towards the west."

"We are offering water to the departed', said the priest, to quench their thirst".

'Then I am offering water to my parched croplands in Punjab' said the Guru.

The priest laughed and said, "How can you do that?" The Guru paused as a crowd gathered around to watch the scene. The Guru then asked, "How far are your ancestors?".

"Forty nine crore kos", the priest replied. "My place is five hundred kos only," Guru Nanak remarked promptly, "If your water can reach crores of kos, then why can't my water reach five hundred kos?".

Priest had no reply. Guru Nanak further said,"You want to send water to those who have no thirst as they are beyond it. My fields require water badly". The people laughed aloud. They understood the gimmicks of the priest.

Guru Nanak then explained them the uselessness of having ritual baths. He Said 'Man may perform lip recitations, austerities, and self restraint and dwell at places of pilgrimage. He may give donations and alms and do other good deeds, but it is useless, if His Name does not dwell in the heart'.[2] Guru Nanak then went to camping area. 'There he was invited by priests for meals. They did special cleaning of the area by plastering the place with mud, drawing a line around'[3].

The Guru Nanak asked Mardana to cook the meals. When Mardana went to take fire from the pandits they fell upon him. The story is well described in verse.

'And hear again, at Hardwar's fair and nook,
Nanak asked Mardana, to fetch fire to cook.
The orthodox around when his pots were touched
Fell upon Mardana, saying, "I will bring you to book".
Nanak thought and very gently so said,
"Evil and hatred are in his heart and head.
Purity lies in inner-self not fire and pots.
Divinity resides not in objects but soul instead"[4]
Guruji explained to the pandits:-

(*Jooth na raagi, Jooth na vedi*[5] pp. 1233).

"There is no impurity in the different phases of the moon and the sun. There is no impurity in music nor there is any impurity in Vedas. There is no impurity in the different phases of the moon and the sun. There is no impurity in the corn, nor is impurity in ablution. There is no impurity in the rain, nor any impurity in water. No impurity is contained in the air either, says Nanak, there is no virtue in the man, without the Guru. If he turns his face away, the mouth is defiled then.[6]"

Guruji then explained to them

(*Kubudh Doomni, Kudcia kasain*'[7] p.97)

"Evil intellect is the she-drummer; heartlessness, the butcheress; slanderer of the heart; the sweeperess, deceitful wart, and a pariat woman what for do you draw lines around, if all these four are seated with you? Make righteousness thy abstenance pious way of life thy lines and Lord's Name thy ablution. Nanak says, these only shall be exquisite who do not tread the path of sin".

Guru Nanak described the limitless powers of the Lord (*Sabhe Surti Yog Sabh*)[8].

'All meditation, all the study of Vedas and Purnas, all are thy deeds. All penances, all songs and all wisdoms, all intellects, all ingenuities, all religious places, all rules, all authority, all joys and all delicacies, all mortals, all deities, all unions and all inclinations, all the worlds, all the continents and all the beings of the universe, all of them, The Lord moves according to His Will and his pen directs our deeds. Nanak says, true is the Lord. True is His Name. True is His congregation and true is His Court"[9].

Some of the people had come to Hardwar to submerge the remains of their dead into Ganges. Priests dragged them too in worthless rituals like that of throwing water back to the river in the name of the dead. Guruji did not approve of this and said (*Nanak chulia suchia je bhar jaane koe*)[10]

"Water taken for sipping is worth, if the real worth of the water itself is known. For the wise man the sipping is of true knowledge and for the yogi it is of chastity. For the Brahaman it is of contentment, and for the householder, of truth and

GURU NANAK THROUGH UTTRAKHAND

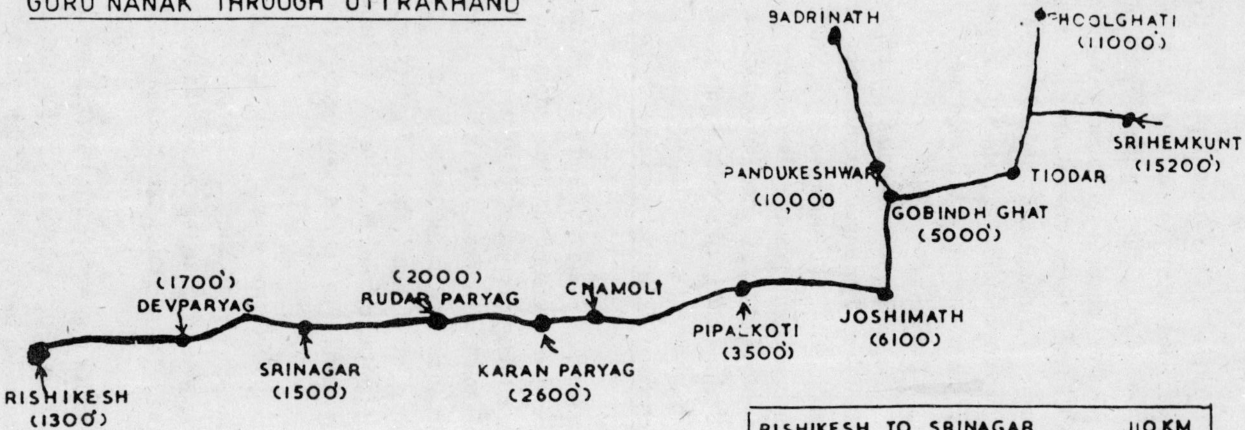

RISHIKESH TO SRINAGAR	110 KM
SRINAGAR TO GOVIND GHAT	159 "
GOVIND GHAT TO SRI HEMKUNT	13 "
GOVIND GHAT TO BADRINATH	13 "
GHAGRIYA TO PHOOLGHATI	1.5 "
RISHIKESH TO HEMKUNT	280 "

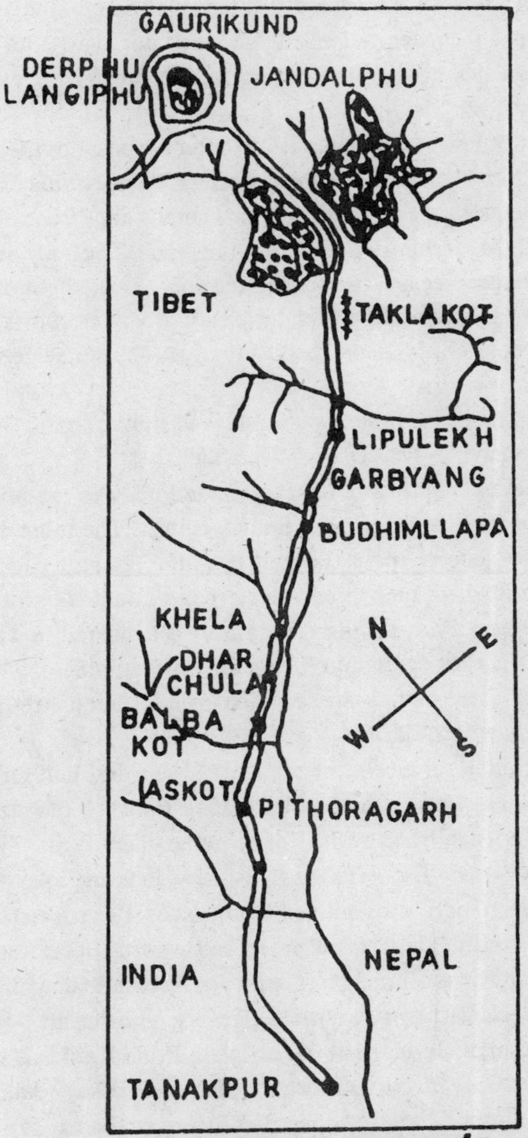

GURU NANAK'S
ROUTE TO KAILASH

> charity. For the kingship, it is of justice and for the learned man it is of concentration. Water does not wash the heart, but quenches thirst. The water is the creater as well as the destroyer".

He saw a few men in melancholy after desposal of the remains of their dead. Guru Nanak calmed them saying, "*Nanak dunia bhas rang*"[11].

> 'Nanak says the world is of ash colour and becomes ash at its end. All earning from this ash is ash too. The body dealing with ash becomes ash itself when the soul is taken out of the body, only ash remains. After his death when mortal is asked the account of his deeds, the resultant is ash and he gets ten times ash in return".

As they mourned in sorrow and showed signs of pain, Guru Nanak solaced them saying, (*Dukh Vich Jamana*)[12].

> 'A man is born and dies in pain and he lives too in pain. Pain after-pain is suffering of human beings. The more one tries to know about the pain, the more he wails. The pain packet is loose, out of which no happiness emerges. A man is burnt after pain and he leaves wailing. Those who get insured in True Lord's praise, they come into life again with happiness, with the fire in pain, the mortals are scorched to death, but it is the pain alone which cures all ills'.

Guru Nanak stayed for the night about one and half furlong from Harki pauri. 'The place is now called Nanak Bara. A life-sized-idol of Guru Nanak is established by the Udasis in the dharamsala. Swami Sant Ram, a follower of Baba Bhagwan is now looking after the place. Gurdwara Gian Godri also commemmorates Guru's visit to Hardwar'[13].

From Hardwar Guru Nanak proceeded towards Badri Nath through Kankhal, Kotdwar and Srinagar (Garhwal). At Kankhal again the Guru held discussions with yogis. Nirmla Panthis, Panchayati Akhada and Satighat remind of Guru's visit these places. From Kankhal, he went to Kotdwar. There is an old Gurdwara (Charan Padika) reminiscent of Guru's visit. From Kotdwar he reached Srinagar (Pauri Garhwal).

Srinagar (Garhwal)

At Srinagar Garhwal, Guru Nanak stayed near the place of Raja Ajaipal the then ruler. A Gurdwara'Charan Padika' was first constructed to commemmorate the visit. It was washed away by flooded Alaknanda in the Year 1803. A new Gurdwara has been constructed at a distance from the place now'[14]. From Srinagar, Guru Nanak visited Badri Nath. At Badrinath, there is a Dharamsala in the name of Guru, From Badrinath, Guru" is said to have gone to Basudhar and Hemkunt. There from, he proceeded to Kailash, Mansarover and held discussions with Sidhs. He returned to Pithoragarh of Uttar-Khand through Taklakot, Lipulekh, Sangchum, Kalapani, Nirpain, Galaghar, Tithila, Khela, Dharchula, Balbakot and Askot. From Pithoragrh, he proceeded to Bageshwar[15].

Bageshwar

'He reached Bageshwar where there is a platform with an inscription and Nishan (flag) commemmorating Guru's visit near Bageshwar[16].'

Almora

'From Bageshwar he proceeded to Almora. At this place, the Raja desired to present Mardana as a sacrifice to the Goddess, but was saved by the Guru. There is now a Gurdwara at this place'[17]. From Almora District the Guru entered Nainital district and attended the fair at Garh-Mukteshwar and passed through Nainital.

Nainital

'There is a platform at about 3 K.Ms from Nainital which is known as Nanak Thara. From Nainital Guru Nanak Proceeded to Kashipur'[18]. Gurudwara Nankana Sahib at Kashipur commemmorates Guru's visit to this place. The Guru stayed at this place for some time. Guru's next halt was Haldwani.

Haldwani

'A few miles from Haldwani, there is a Ber Tree under which the Guru is said to have rested a while. It is held in his sacred memory'[19].

Nanak Matta

'From Haldwani Guruji Proceeded to Gorakhmata which now is known as Nanak Matta'[20]. The Guru went to the places of residence of yogis and sat under a peepal tree nearby . The tree bacame green with Guru's touch. It was winter. At night it became extremely cold. Guru Nanak sent one of his companions to fetch fire from the Yogis. Yogis feeling humiliated by Guru's followership, refused to give fire and remarked, 'Ask your Guru to produce fire himself'. Guru, hearing of this, kept cool. Soonafter a great storm arose. All the fire of yogis was extinguished and a big fire began to burn near the Guru. Yogis felt the bite of the cold and came running to Guru Nanak for the fire. The Guru asked them to take fire by leaving their earrings and wooden sandles as pawn.

In the morning, the Yogis assembled with a view to subdue the Guru. The yogis questioned the Guru, "*Kaun tarazi kaun tula*'[21].

> 'What scales and weights art thou efficacy and who is thou assayer?' From which Guru did you receive instructions and who appraises your worth?'.

Guru Nanak looked up towards God and replied,

> "My God, My venerable beloved, you are the limitless. Thou art fully contained in water, dry land, nether and upper regions. Thou thyself art pervading everywhere. My soul is the scale the consciousness, the weight and the performance of the jeweller. O Lord, O My spouse, weigh me from my innerself which I keep attached to you. Thou thyself art the tongue of the balance, the weights and the balance. Thou thyself art the weighman. Thou Thyself beholdest Thyself, Thou understatdest and Thou Thyself art ehe dealer. The blind the low cast, the strantger soul comes for a moment and departs in a trice. Nanak abides in Your companionship. Thus, 'O' Lord which the Unexperienced cannot attain'[22].

The Yogis asked Guru Nanak, 'why don't you become a yogi and wear dress as ours?'.

Guru Nanak replied, '*Jog na khintha jog na dandai, jog no bhasam charhaiye*'[23]

> 'Yog lies not in begging bowl, in carrying a staff, nor in smearing the limbs with ashes,
> Yoga lies not in earrings or in cropping the hair close, or in blowing the horn.
> To live immaculate amidst the impurities of the world. This is true Yoga-practice'[24].

Yogis feeling defeated, planned a few miracles. First, they tried to lift the peepal tree in the air. As the tree was lifted about 5 feet from the ground, the Guru made a sign towards the tree to stop. The tree stood there and then and is still there till today. Later on, a platform was built around the roots. The site on which the tree stands is known as 'Panjabi' by the old inhabitants of Uttar Pradesh.

The yogis did not stop at that. They began to show miracles one after the other to tease and trouble Guru Nanak. The Guru realised that these yogis required some other treatments as they paid no heed to discussions and their ego was sky high. The Guru ordered his wooden sandal (Khadav) to give them good beating. Finally, subdued by the beating by the Khadav, the yogis fell on Guru's feet for their safety. The Guru asked them to be humane and egoless and to stop all miracles as these distracted their mind from spiritual development. Almost all the yogis came to senses but some of the yogis feeling hurt, performed another miracle. They dried up water of all the wells of the area and requested the Guru, for the water for their bath. The guru gave his stick to Mardana and asked him to draw a line from the river to the place without break. He also advised him not to look back. Mardana did as instructed, but when he was about 2 furlongs from the Guru, he looked behind, wondering as to what was happening. He was astonished to find the river following him. His looking back stopped the river wherever it was. The Guru then, asked the yogis to bring the river up to his seat. They tried but could do nothing. He then, asked them to see if the water had come to their wells. Lo! all the wells were full of water.

The streamlet is now part of 'Nanak Sagar' and the sacred well near the Guru's resting place has been truned into a Baoli amidst Nanak Sagar and is connected with the banks through a bridge.

The peeple tree which was burnt by the jealous yogis sprout forth new leaves when the Sixth Guru sprinkled water mixed with saffron. Local Sikhs (Tharus) have great reverence for the place and consider wood ash from Guru ka langar as sacred.

Reetha Sahib

'From Gorkhmatta (Now called Nanak Matta) Guru Nanak proceeded to a place now known as Reetha sahib'[25].

Mardana feeling hungry as usual requested food from yogis. These yogis had heard about Guru's ordeal with yogis at Nanak Matta. In anger they told Mardana, 'We have no food for you. Why don't you ask your Guru to produce the same?'. The Guru overheard this. He asked Mardana to climb a soapnut tree in the vicinity and to enjoy the food. Soapnut is too bitter for consumption. But when Mardana started eating the soapnuts, he found these too tasty. Mardana had his fill. Yogis, astonished at this, wanted to taste the fruit for themselves but found it too bitter. Infact, the side of the tree from which Mardana plucked fruit is sweet till date while the other side wherefrom yogis plucked, is bitter. Some seeds of a sweeter side were taken and sown at a different place and later a group of trees grew with sweet Soapnuts. These trees are known as 'Nanak Bagichi'. The tree from which the sweet soapnuts were eaten by Mardana is known as 'Reetha Sahib'.

Tanda

'From Reetha Sahib, Guru Nanak proceeded to Bareilly and then to Tanda. This town was primarily of traders. Guru Nanak sat down near a trader's house where celebrations were going on. Lot of people were coming to the trader's house. Mardana wanted to know why there was so big a gathering? Further he felt hungry as usual. He enquired from the passers-by about it and was told that the trader was blessed with a son. Mardana requested Guru Nanak, "Please permit me to go to trader's house and to congratulate him on his son's birthday. If you wish I can get somthing to eat for you as well". Guru Nanak replied. "He is not blessed with a son but a creditor, who after staying for a day will go back. If you wish to go then you just go, stand and watch without saying a word". Mardana proceeded to the place. However, no one bothered for Mardana; hence he returned.

After sometime, the child expired, Guru Nanak then sang a Shabad[26]. *(Pahile pahrai rain kai, vanjariya mitra, Hukami paiya garbhas).*

> 'In the first quarter of the night, my Merchant-Friend, by Divine Will wast thou cast into the womb; Suspended by the head, didst thou undergo penance, there in supplicating the Master for release. Suspended downward didst thou supplicate and absorb thy thought in the Master. Comest thou in shame into the world; unclad shalt thou return. Man gets what is writ in his destiny, Saith Nanak, in the first quarter was man cast in the womb.

(dujai pahrai rayan kai vanjariya mitra visar gaya dhiyan).

> In the second quarter of night, Merchant-friend, hast thou put God out of mind. By diverse hand wast thou founded with love as Kishan in the home of Yasoda. By diverse hands fondled, thou bubble of breath, thy mother showered love on thee; think, think thou involved in forgetfulness, shall last with thee; He who created thee, Him hast thou forgotten Contemplate Him with thy mind. Saith Nanak, in the second quarter hast thou put God out of mind.

(tijai pahrai rayan kai vanjariya mitra dhan joban siun chitt)

> In the third quarter of night, Merchant-friend, thy heart on wealth and desire is fixed. Though thinkst not of God, liberator from bondage. Forgetful of God, thou, wanderst in Maya's maze. Lured by wealth and drunk in desire, thou hast cast thy life away. Thy merchandise has not been Right eouseness, nor Friend, you have engaged in good deeds. Saith Nanak, in the third quarter is man absorbed in wealth and desire.

(chauthai pahrai rayan kai vanjariya mitra lavi aiya khet)

In the fourth quarter of night, the reaper comes to the field, led by Yama's minions, merchant-friend, none thy destination knows in the grip of Yama's minions, none knowth the why or where. Victims of illusion would cry round the bier in a moment wouldst thou, a stranger, be as thy desire in life. Saith Nanak; Listen, thou man, in the fourth quarter the reaper comes to reap the field.'

The traders gathered around the Guru and heard the Shabad. They soon understood the uselessness of rituals and worried about the materialistic world. They became Guru's followers. Guru Nanak stayed there for some days; then proceeded through Pilibhit and Kheri Districts and reached Kohri-Wala-Ghat.

Kohriwala Ghat

Kohriwala Ghat, now known as Koiralaghat was visited by Guru Nanak for the sake of the leper, who remembered the Guru with great faith and devotion. Guru redeemed him and gave him the True name. Therefrom, he proceeded to Ayodhya Nemisharniya in Sitapur district, a Hindu pilgrimage centre.

Ayodhya

Ayodhya was the ancient Kingdom of legendry Lord Rama, 'Guru Nanak held discussions with the pandits on the bank of Saryu river'[27]. The haughty materialistic pandits believed more in rituals in meditation. Guru told them their characterstics as follows:-

(pad pustak sandhya badang)[28]

'You read books, say vesper prayers, argue, worship stones and sit in trance like crane. With your mouth you utter falsehood like the excellent ornaments....but He Himself is the Immaculate Lord'(p.1345)

Guru Nanak explained them as to who a true Brahmin is. He said, *"So brahman jo binde brahm"*[29]. 'He alone is a true Brahmin who knows the Transcendent Lord; who does the penance, has self restraint and has true devotion to the Lord; who observes the faith of humility and contentment and who is capable of breaking his bones to get emancipated'.

Guru Nanak further described *(Jagan hom pun jap puja)*[30]

'Even though man may give gratutious feasts, do yoga, offer alms, perform penance and worship and endure bodily pain and suffer but without Lord's Name, he does not attain emancipation and is never redeemed. His name is attained by the Guru's grace. Without the Lord's Name. One's birth in this world is in vain. Without Lord's Name, man eats poison, utters poisonous words and dies an improfitable death and wonders after death.'[31]

On being asked by Mardana about the importance of Ayodhya, the Guru described the story of Rama and the scene of battle between Rama and the Ravana *(Ram jhure dal melvai)*

'With his mind's great power, Ram Chander sadly gathers his army. The army of monkeys was at his service and with his body and soul, he had to become desirous of war. Ten headed Ravana had taken Sita, his wife and Lakshman was affected by the curse. Nanak, the Creater Lord is the doer of all deeds. He creates and destroys Ram Chandra mourned for Sita and Lakshman. He remembered Hanuman, the Monkey God who came to his service. The misguided demon Ravana, does not know that God's ways are strange. Nanak says the ineffaceable are the past deeds which he, the carefree, rewards or punishes"[32].

The pandits realised the truth. They became followers of Guru Nanak. A gurudwara named 'Braham Kund' was constructed on the bank of Saryu river in honour of Guru Nanak's visit. Guru Tegh Bahadur and Guru Gobind Singh too, visited this place later. The gurudwara is now affected by the water of the river Saryu and needs urgent attention for safety from erosion.

Gorakhpur

Guru Nanak proceeded to Gorakhpur from Ayodhya. 'Here he held discussions with yogis again. The yogis were impressed and they became disciples of Guru Nanak. A Dharamsala was built at the place of discussion. Guru's Shabads were sung regularly thereafter'.[33]

From Gorakhpur, Guru Nanak entered Deoria. 'About 5 Km from Deoria there is a memorial commemmorating Guru's visit'[34]. From Gorakhpur he proceeded to Nepal.

References

1. Manfred Garner and Ahluwalia, H.P.S (Maj) : Himalaya : A Practical Guide, New Delhi Himalayan Books, 1985, P. 224-234.
2. *Puratan Janam Sakhi* : P. 52.
3. Kripal Singh (Dr.) : *Janam Sakhi Prampra : Meharban Wali Janam Sakhi,* P. 99
4. Varma Sharad Chander : *Guru Nanak and Logos of Divine Manifestation,* P. 19
5. *Puratan Janam Sakhi :* P. 54.
6. Ibid.
7. Kirpal Singh Dr (Ed): *Janam Sakhi Prampara* : P.37.
8. *Sri Guru Granth Sahib,* P. 1241.
9. *Puratan Janamsakhi* (ed) : Shamsher Singh Ashok, P. 52-55.
10. *Sri Guru Granth Sahib,* P. 1240.
11. Ibid.
12. *Sri Guru Granth Sahib,* P. 1233.
13. Kirpal Singh Dr (ed) : *Janamsakhi Prampara,* P. 37.
14. Pandit Tara Hari Narrotam : *Sri Guru Tirath Sangreh,* P.12.
15. Kirpal Singh Dr. (ed). *Janamsakhi Prampara,* P.37.
16. Ganda Singh Dr. (ed); *Sources on the Life & Teachings of Guru Nanak,* Punjabi University, Patiala, P. 197.
17. Surinder Singh Kohli Dr. : *Travels of Guru Nanak,* P. 31.
18. Ibid.
19. Ibid.
20. Ibid.
21. *Puratan Janam Sakhi,* P.58.
22. *Sri Guru Granth Sahib,* P. 730.
23. *Puratan Janamsakhi* (ed) : Shamsher Singh Ashok, P.58.
24. *Sri Guru Granth Sahib,* P. 730.
25. Kirpal Singh Dr. (ed) : *Janamsakhi Prampara.* 39.
26. *Sri Guru Granth Sahib,* P.74-77.
27. Kirpal Singh Dr. (ed) : *Janamsakhi Prampara* : P.46.
28. *Sri Guru Granth Sahib* : P. 1345.
29. Op Cit P. 1141.
30. Kirpal Singh ed. *Janamsakhi Prampara,* P.46.
31. *Sri Guru Granth Sahib,* P. 1127.
32. Op Cit, P.1412.
33. Surinder Singh Kohli (Dr) : *Travels of Guru Nanak,* P.34.
34. Lal Singh Giani : *Guru Khalsa Twarikh* : P.103.

Tibet

Tibet, the land of Lamas, is situated in the Trans-Himalayan Region bordered by India, Nepal, and Bhutan in the south and west and China in the north and east. 'It is spread over an area of 4,70.000 sq miles of mountainous plateau. Recently under Chinese rule and known as Tibet Autonomous Region, it had been a soveerign state till the occupation by the Chinese in 1951. The average elevation above sea-level is about 13,000 feet. It is practically surrounded by huge mountain ranges'.[1]

Although these physical factors kept it isolated from its neighbours, the Tibetans developed contact and established culturalities with the Northern pastoral population of Mangolia and China and also with India. 'In fact, it had the maximum impact from India. Tibetan script is obtained from India (Originally Brahmi Script), Tibetan religion is obtained from India (Budhism) and the Tibetan calander too, is originated from Indian Book (Kalchakra). The first ruler of Tibet is said to be an Indian from Magadha'.[2]

Before Budhism, people followed Bonism where animal sacrifice and magic played a great role. Budhism entered Tibet in the fifth century, but for the first two hundred years, its impact was not strong. 'In the seventh centry, king Song-Tsen-Gampo gave a firmer footing to Budhism. He founded Lhasa in 639 A.D. and created 180 Budhist temples in Tibet and invited scholars from Nepal and India and arranged for translations of Buddhhist Scriptures'.[3]

Gradually over a period of six hundred years, Tibetan religion got various forms and the sects formed were

(i) rNying-ma-pa
(ii) bKa-ngyud-pa
(iii) Sa-Skya-pa and
(iv) dGe-Lugs-pa.

The Sakya monastry was established in 1073 A.D. by a noble family known as Khon. bKa-nGyud-pa built a monastry in Tshel, rNying-ma-pa also built their monastries at several pleaces out of which Samya Monastry was the main. An Indian, Dipankar Srijnana, known as Atisha, founded bKa-gDam-pa order.

'After the rise of these religious orders, few chieftains who were ruling in various parts of Tibet tried to patronise different sects in order to gain their support'[4].'The Sa-sKya-pa had an abbot who was assisted by a civil and a Military Governor. The bKa-nGyud-pa, too, modelled their administration on a similar pattern'[5].

In 1247, the hereditary abbot of the Sa-sKya-pa was recognised by the Mangols as the highest authority in Tibet. Sa-sKya were overthrown by King Chenchub Gyaltsen (dByang-Chub-nGyaltsen)[6] who was a bKa-gDam-pa, an offshoot of nGying-Ma-Pa sect.

In the latter part of the fourteenth century, an eminent religious leader, Tsong-Kha-Pa, established a new sect known as 'dGe-Lugs-Pa' or the 'Yellow Hats'. In 'dGe-Lugs-Pa' sect, practice of reincarnation started after the death of a successor of Tsong-Kha-Pa. The third successor and reincarnation, Sonam Gyatso (Sonam-nGyatso) spread the new faith in Mongolia and received the title Dalai Lama Vajradhara from the Mongol ruler Altan Khan'[7].

The dGe-Lugs-Pa had built three large monastries, the Sera, the Garden and the Drepung. Some dGe-Lugs-pa monastries were built at Chamdo in Kham and Tashilhunpo in Tsang, inspite of Karma-pa predomiance in these areas. Very often, there were battles between these camps. 'Monastries were not only the centres of meditation or learning but also of administration and power. These chief monastries became the centres of power struggle until rise of temporal power of dGe-Lugs-Pa by the beginning of 15th century,[8] the time of visit of Guru Nanak to Tibet.

Guru Nanak's faith spread well in Red Hat Sects of which the Kar-Ma-Pa sect was the strongest. Guru Nanak's advent on the scene of this struggle when the Red Hats were persecuted was of great importance. They found in Guru Nanak, a saviour, a helper in times of need; hence, their faith in Guru Nanak deepened further. Kar-Ma-Pas (Nying-Ma-Pa) follow Mahansandhi, a book which contains same or nearly the same cantos (Pauris) in Tibetan, as that of Japuji. However, Dalai Lama and dGe-Lugs-Pa sect remained away from the influence of Guru Nanak. If Red hats would have been the rulers, there was no doubt that Guru Nanak's place would have been in the state religion in Tibet.The influence was restricted due to dGe-Lugs-Pa predominance of Central and Northern regions. However, Guru Nanak is worshipped by multitudes of Red Hats in Western and Southern Tibet as well as amongst Red Hats settled in Nepal, Sikkim, Bhutan and Arunachal Pradesh.

Guru Nanak came in contact with the Lamas at Rawalsar, in the beginning of Sumer Udasi. His impact on these Lamas was instant. Lamas accepted Guru's leadership after subjugation of these Sidhs who were a great religious force in Western Tibet. This had a direct impact on the pilgrims who had come to Sumer from different parts of Tibet.

Guru Nanak is said to have visited Tibet six times i.e. from four different areas during his Udasi to the North East. 'First time, he visited Tibet while visiting Sumer (Kailash)'[9] 'Second time, he crossed into Tibet from Nepal and after visiting Sakya-Pa monastry entered Sikkim. Third time, he entered Chumbi valley of Tibet while crossing into Bhutan. Fourth time, he went to Lhasa and Samya Monastry from Twang (Arunachal) and fifth time, he went from Menchukha (Arunachal Pradesh) to Tuting-Gelling valleys through Tibet and got a tribe (Membas) settled in Menchukha and Tuting-Gelling valleys' [10]. His sixth visit is during his return from China through Tibet where from he went to Ladakh-Kashmir.

His visit to Kailash is well described in Janmsakhis and also by Bhai Gurdas, Giani Gyan Singh, Giani Lal Singh and Dr. S.S. Kohli. However the visits to other Himalayan region are not well described, references are available in Giani Gyan Singh's 'Panth Prakash' by and in Dr. Tarlochan Singh's book 'Jeevan Charit Guru Nanak Dev' and Dr. Surinder Singh Kohli's book 'Travels of Guru Nanak'.

The author during his travels to the Himalayan states and in discussions with Lamas and Tibetans settled in India, has been able to reconstruct the details about the routes adopted by Guru Nanak to Tibet; the same details are given in succeeding paragraphs.

Kailash-Mansarover

Guru Nanak entered Kailash-Mansarovar area of Tibet from Uttar Pradesh's Garhwal region (Uttarkhand). From Rishikesh, he went through Devprayag, Srinagar (Garhwal), Rudarprayag, Daras and Uttrakashi and reached Gangotri. From Gangotri, he went to Gaumukh and visited Tapovan. From Tapovan, he went through Manna Pass and reached Kailash region, where Siddh's had established themselves.

For thousands of years, the Kailash-Mansarovar area has been held sacred by Hindus, Buddhists and the followers of Bon, Tibet's indigenous religion. Even today, pilgrims carry out devotional circumbulations there and converge on Mount Kailash by pilgrim paths from all over Tibet and India. Hindus consider Kailash to be Lord Shiva's throne. Lord Shiva sits in eternal, at Kailash the long strands of his matted hair falling and flowing all about him, The mighty Brahmaputra and holy Ganges are said to emante from some of these strands.

Buddhist cosmography, identifies Kailash with the mighty Mount Sumeru, central peak of the world. Holy lake Mansarovar, the "Mother Pearl" represents Buddhist transcendent, consciousness. The 'father-mountain' itself represents the means to enlightenment.

As a Bon centre, Mount Kailash has enjoyed great popularity in the folk religion of Tibet. It is the soul of the country and assures perpetuity and protection for all the Tibetan people.

Physically, too, the area is outstanding. At 6714 metres (22022 ft), Mount Kailash is one of the highest mountains in Western Tibet. Lake Mansarovar is generally recognised as the highest body of fresh water in the world. The Indus, Sutlej, Ganges and Yarlong Tsangpo (Brahmaputra) rivers, the vital waterways for Tibet and South Asia; all originate from and around Mount Kailash.

The main local town is Burang (Taklakot) 110 km south of Mount Kailash. It is in the Ngari (Ali) District of Western Tibet, its administrative centre being at the town of Shiquanha 250 km west of Mount Kailash on the road to Xinjiang.

At Kailash

After reaching Sumeru peak of Kailash, "Guru Nanak met the 84

Sidhs, the desciples of Gorakh Nath"[11]. These men of miracles sat on their seats forming an assembly. As the Guru approached them they said to him, {"*Sidh sabha kar asan baithe*"(p-938)}, "Make thou salutaion to this assembly of Saints".

Guru Nanak answered, "My salutation is to Him alone, Him, who is True, Infinite and extremely Exquisite. I cut off my head and lay it before him and surrender my body and soul to Him. By His blessings only, we attain the true glory"[12].

The miracle men were astonished at Guru Nanak's behaviour. They requested Guru Nanak to disclose his name, sect, object of life, seat and whom he followed. Guru Nanak replied, "My name is Nanak. I have come from God. In Him is my seat and in Him is my abode. My seat is to remain according to His will. My way is to reside in the Imperishable Lords' contemplative mood and the attainment of such a transcendental comtemplation is my life's object".

"Where do you come from and where do you go?" asked Sidhs. "I have emerged from God and will go where He directs me to. I wish to be one with Him by knowing and recognising Him and myself by Guru's Grace", answered Guru Nanak. Sidhs became curious. "How can you cross this impassable worldocean like this?" they enquired.

"As a lotus remains unaffected in water and duck swims against the stream's current without getting wet, I remain untouched from worldly feelings, with the kind guidance of my teacher and by uttering Lord's name as guided." spoke Guru Nanak, "World's beginning is a great wonder. The great Lord lives everywhere in everyone's heart and within-self too".

Yogis proceeded with questions, "How can death stroke be fended off and how can one enter the home of fearlessness? How can the evil adverseries be slain?".

Guru Nanak explained, "If one realises His Name; the one who created the universe, then death, instead of striking him becomes his slave. If a man knows the God, the seat of true bliss and contentment; and through Guru's word, 'effaces his ego, sin and evil', then he abides in his own home of fearlessness. The one who works for the Lord and serves no one else, he finds his way to slay his evils, the adversaries".

Impressed by Guru's answer, Sidhs found him capable of clearing their doubts. They asked him the way of attainment of the God. "How can we reach The Great God's gates?" Guru Nanak replied, "By uttering His name, one reaches at His Gates, enters His seat and Unites with Him".

Loharipa a disciple of Gorakh stated Sidhs method of attainment of enlightenment, "We live in jungles, fully detached from the world and survive on fruits and roots. We keep ourselves clean by having bath in sacred rivers and have no filth on our body. By keeping ourselves clean we do yoga to be one with Him".

Guru Nanak did not approve of this and said, "Yoga is not cleaning of the body Mere. Sitting in yoga posture and keeping awake and hungry is to create problem for the body by. Actual Yoga is to keep one's mind and heart clean. It is true Yoga if you renounce all egos and worldly attachments and discard lust, wrath and self-conceit and connect your mind to The One. When the Teacher's instructions guide you to Him you shall see that God is everywhere and by pleasing Him you shall be able to attain the venerable position of being with Him".

Sidhs were still under the mist of their worldly knowledge and were unable to grasp the truth. They still questioned. "Who is that unmanifest who emancipates? What is that which goes from us and what comes in? Who is prevailing upon all the three worlds?"

Guru Nanak answered coolly, "He who permeates all the hearts is unmanifest. The follower of the True Master is emancipated and is united with God's name both from within and without. The egos are bound to come and go but it is the True Lord, who always prevents one from all the three worlds". Yogis had doubts about 'maya'. They asked, "How is one bound and subdued by God of Mammon? How does a man get lost with it and how to gain from it? How can we be pure and become enlightened?".

Guru Nanak explained," The God of Mammon subdues persons due to human folly of attachment to worldly things. The apostate loses from the world but the pious person gains from the world as he follows the True Teacher and dispels the attraction of the worldly affairs. He kills the ego and becomes pure, gets enlightened and merges with The One".

Yogis doubted Guru's basics of becoming a Yogi and questioned about his dress, manners etc. Guru Nanak dispelled their doubts by stating," I became a hermit in search of true saints and have worn the special dress to cause curiosity even for The God. I have to trade true merchandise and by Guru's grace I shall be able to ferry my sect across".

Yogis were astonished at Guru's ways of life and were eager to know with whom he had united his soul. They also wanted to know how he got the true light from within as it is just like eating iron without teeth.

Guru Nanak answered,"By dwelling in true Guru's own mind, my life's course is changed and my mind wanders no more, as it is attached to the celestial string. With the help of The God's Name, I have burnt my desire and hope and by Guru's grace I have found the light within me. I have been able to eat even iron of difficulty by effacing the three i.e. desire, hope and ego".

"How did the world come into existence? Where does the creater reside and who is he actually, who is everywhere and in each heart?" The yogis asked further, to which Guru Nanak replied.

"As for the beginning of the world, one can only think and talk in terms of wonder. The profound Lord, then did dwell within His Ownself. The True Lord, the life of all, abides within all the hearts".

Yogis questioned further, "Wherefrom has the man come? Where does he go and wherein remains he merged?.

Guru Nanak explained,"The man originates from Lord's command. He goes back to where His Will is and he remains merged in His Will".

Guru Nanak first explained the meaning of Guru, as "He who understands the meaning of His Divine Discourse". Thereafter Guru answered the other questions. "By means of Guru's words; man easily obtains and merges in the pure formless reality by practising truth and realising Lord's dignity and worth; he is blessed with the Lord's love by the perfect Guru. Wonderous is the Will of Him, Who Himself is the Destroyer and Creater. He alone knows His command and truely understands the way of life of the beings.

The Siddhs then asked about the moral standards in the world. Guru Nanak explained the standards of these worldly values as follows:-

(Sati pap kar Sat Kamaveh)[13].

'The men in charity, give in charity the wealth amassed by

committing sins. Their Guru goes to their home to impart instructions. The Woman loves the man for his money otherwise she cares not wherefrom he comes and where to he goes. No body obeys the Shashtras and the Vedas. Everyone worships but himself. A Qazi is a judge who tells the rosary muttering God's Name, but takes bribe and does injustice openly. If someone askes him, he quotes and reads out some aphorsia. The Muslim creed permeates the ears and hearts of Hindus. They plunder people and indulge in backbiting. Hindus plaster their cooking square to become pure. This is the state of Hindus"[14].

Siddhs wanted to know conditions in the world as prevalent then. Guru Nanak said (Such Kal Kood Vartia)[15]

"There is a famine of truth. Falsehood prevails and the dark age has made men demons. Those who had sown the seed of the Name, departed with honour, but the seed is left broken which cannot sprout again. If the seed be wholesome and there be the proper season; then only the seed will germinate". Nanak says,"Without a mordant, the brand new cloth cannot be dyed. If the mordant of modesty be applied to the sins, they can be washed away with Lord's fear, making the body and heart clean", Nanak further says, "If the man be imbued with the Lord's meditation, then his reputation is not at all false"[16].

Guru Nanak explained further *(Lab Pap doe raja Mehta Koor Hoya Sikdar)*[17].

"The avarice and sin are the King and Minister and falsehood is the master of mint. Lust, the assistant official who is the chief consultant. They all sit together and chalk out evil plans. The blind public is without wisdom who satisfies the official's fire of greed with bribe. The learned play music and dance to their tune and show off falsehood! They shout aloud and sing epic poems and hero's tales. The fools call themselves scholars and amass wealth through cunning. The virtuous disguise their meritorious acts by asking for the door of salvation and leave their home and hearth for meditation, the method of which is not known to them. Every one considers himself perfect. None calls himself wanting. If the weight of honour is put into the hind scale, then alone, O Nanak, the man appears properly weighed".[18]

Guruji Then said *(Kal Kati Raje Kasai),*[19]

'The dark age is the sealpel, the kings are the butchers and righteousness has attained wings and flown. In this dark night of falsehood, the moon of truth is not seen to rise anywhere. In search of God, hearts have become bewildered in darkness. I find no path by taking pride; mortals bewail in pain'[20].

Sidhs found Guru Nanak highly knowledgeable about the Lord. They thought, 'Our religion can find great advancement through him; hence let us make him accept our followship'. However, they were eager to test his virtues. They asked him to bring water from the lake. As Guru Nanak put the earthern pot into the lake, he found it full with jewels. This was due to magic spell by the Yogis. Guru Nanak broke the small earthen pot and joined the broken pieces again thereby breaking the magic spell. He was able to fill the water into the newly joined pot, which he took to the Sidhs. They were surprised at Guru's fete. Astonishingly the water from the small earthen pot turned out to be suffcient to quench the thrst of all the Sidhs around! The Sidhs were highly impressed at Guru's achievement'[21]. They then asked him, "Are you a householder or renunciater?". Guru explained to them as to who is a true householder, who is truely detached and who is a true renunciator. He also explained them as to who is a disguiser and desireless[22]. Then he told them, "Outer appearances are deceptive. It is one's innerself which must be clean and tuned to the God even when one is a householder". Guru explained this thus, "He alone is the householder who checks his passion and does meditation during hard toil. He gives charity and alms from what he earns through his personal efforts. He is a pure householder as is the water of the Ganges. The Lord is the embodiment of the truth. He who has no form or shape is the Supreme reality".

Guru Nanak then explained the characteristics of a detached person (Udasi);

"He alone is detached who burns conceit himself. He begs the food of self realisation and asks for ams to remain in true abode, the abode of the Lord, where he ultimately resides. Lord is the embodiment of truth. There is no sign, form or shape of the

Supreme Reality". About renunciator, Guru said, "He alone is the renunciator who embraces renunciation. He realises the Immaculate Lord residing in all the regions. He ties knot to both heat of the sun and coolness of the moon. The one who is both cool and hot in one, his body will never fail. Nanak says to Gopi Chand, 'The Lord is the embodiment of the truth. The Supreme Reality has no sign, shape or form".

Then Guru Nanak described a disguiser (Pakhandi).

He said, "He alone is a dis-guiser who washes off filth from his soul. He burns his internal and external fires by God's Name. Even in dream, he controls his outlet. Such a disguiser neither ages nor dies".

He explained the qualities of a desireless Person.

"He alone is desireless who turns towards the Lord. He uses the key of God's Name to open his tenth gate (Dasam Dwar). He remains absorbed in meditation day and night. Such a desireless person is like the true Lord".

'He explained the path of true Yoga and salvation'[23].

(Gur Ka Sabad, Mane Mahi Mundra-P. 259). 'Let Guru's word be the earrings in your mind and wear the patched coat of forbearance. Whatever the Lord does, consider that supreme. Thus you shall easily obtain the treasure of Yoga. The soul thus united is a yogi all the ages through. It is absorbed in the Supreme quitessence. He who has obtained the ambrosal name of the Immaculate Lord; his body enjoys the pleasure of Divine knowledge. He forsakes desires and disputes and sits in contemplative mood in the the Lord's abode. From the heart-horn's sound, an everlasting and beautiful melody abode is produced which day and night fills him with Divine music. Reflection is cup and Divine knowledge his sectarian staff. To abide in Lord's Presence is his end. God's Praise is his vocation and the exalted Guru's way his pure religion. His Chief desire is to see Lord's light amongst all. Lord has numerous colours. Nanak finds Him every where. Hence he professes love only for the Supreme Lord".[24]

As it became the time for their food, the Yogis offered wine to Guru

Nanak and spoke in praise of this wine. Guru Nanak did not approve of this and said (Gud Kar Gian, Dhian Kar Dhavai)[25].

"Make gnosis your mollasses and meditation your flowers of basia latifolia. In them, put good deeds as the fermanting bark. Make faith, the furnance and love, the plaster. In this way the sweet nectar is distilled. 'O Yogi' by quaffing the name Nectar, the mind becomes intoxicated and easily remain's absorbed in Lord's love. By fixing attention on God's affection and hearing celestial songs day and night, life becomes fruitful. The perfect one, naturely, gives this cup of truth to drink to him on whom He castes, His merciful glance. Why should he, who is the dealer, of Nectar, embrace love for Paltry wine. The Guru's word is nectar speech. By quaffing it, man becomes acceptable to Him. What should he, who is the lover of Lord's vision, do with salvation and paradise? He who is imbued with God's praise, is ever renowned, who never loses in gamble[26].

Yogis were impressed by Guruji's reply. They said, "We are pleased with you. Ask any boon or whatever you wish". Guruji said, "I have got the boon of God who is Supreme. What else do I want"? He further said, *"(Thapia na Jai, Kita na Hoe)*[27].

'And who can cast in any form your image install?
Self-Existent, Self-Sufficient, beyond material facts, all
Unaided and unconditioned, independent of things mundane,
Autophanour, with cocinty unto Himself and contained,
Nanak sings to treasury of His goodness, all praise to Him,
The mind in absolute communion, lighting sorrows dark-inn
They that truly serve, with all devotion and love, proceed,
By glorifying Him. Behold, in the recesses of the heart,
His love doth dwell and all miseries melt in joyous repast
Thus with mediation intense, in tune with God Himself!
Involutely facing towards the Guru, is enlightenment Itself
The word is Nad, eternal and celestial music of the soul.
This is wisdom of the Vedas, in fact, it's theology whole.
Enlightement is Ishar, Vishnu and Brahma-creation entire.
Enlightement is Parbati and Laksmi; all in same attire.
Indeterminate-beyond expression of thought.

Despite knowing Him. His description is however never got.
And may the Guru give an understanding of this mystery deal
That I never forget Him, the Source-Sustainer of life indeed.
(SGGS, P. 2)

Senior Sidhs still wanted that Guru Nanak must ask for something material. Guruji replied again *(Je Jug Chare Aarja)*[34].

"If human life span spread to encompass ages four,
And its product computed by even a denaryu more,
With following, in nine planets of creation, all the same,
Recognised, renewed, respected; with reverance and fame.
But bereft of gracious, graceful, gentle eye of Lord,
Sinner amongst sinner, worn amongst vermins in creations' lot
Virtue to virtueless bestowed, showered by Him ever more,
Copicus ethical excellence, to those already endowed before,
Memory recalls not, without, or give moral virtues to HIM, at-last.[35]
(S.G.G.S P. 2)

Guruji's discourses with Sidhas were prolonged over a number of days. The Sidhas accepted the superiority of Guru's teachings and in turn, the local people around became Guru's followers. 'There are four Lama-temples at the four corners of Mansarover Lake. All of them have Guru Nanak's idols which are worshipped by them. Footprints of Guruji are still preserved in Shapji on the monastry from the hill resorts of Hippa, Kanan Puha etc, upto Gartok, the route is covered after brief Intervals and the picture of Guru Nanak appears on the ceiling of such coverings'[36].

It is probable that Guruji's victory over Sidhs was the cause of perpetuating Guru's memory in these parts. Guruji also visited Tavchin, Gaurikund, Jandalphu, Derphu and Sandiphu from there.

After visiting Gurlapass, Baldhak, Khotan Nath, Mansarover, Kailash and the neighbouring areas, the Guru returned through Taklakot, Lipulekh, Sangchum, Kalapani, Garbyang, Buddimallppa, Nirpain, Galaghar, Tithila, Khela, Darchula, Balbakot and Askot, to Pithoragarh. From there, Guru proceeded to Almora district. (This was a main route to Mansarover in those days).

Sakya

Guru Nanak's second entry to Tibet was from Nepal. He is said to have gone to Sakya on an invitation from Lamas of Sakya. Nepal-Lhasa Road-link after crossing Nanak La Pass in Himalayan region crosses over to Tinggri Dzong and passes through Lhatse and Shigtse on to Lhasa. Sakya, sacred Budhist monastry in Southern Tibet is situated in between Lhatse and Shingtse, the two largest towns after Lhasa. It is in the richest area of Tibet ie; the outer pleateau. To reach Sakya from Shigtse one has to turn from the main highway to Lhasa, from Sakya River bridge 15 Kms from the top of the Tsuo la Pass, A rough road leads down a long, dry valley from 26 km to Sakya village. Total distance to Sakya frm Shigtse is 128 Kms.

The forbidding, fortress like monastry, can be seen from a distance looking like single grey and red block with one horizontal white strip. The important old monastry, whose name means 'Tawny Soul' governed the whole Tibet in the 13th century, after the downfall of the kings. Originally, the monastry stood in two parts, built at different times, on either side of the river. The first was founded in 1071 by a powerful nobel family of Tsang. Its buildings, incorporating a cave, were raised against the mountain side of east of the river in typical Tibeten style. Much scholarship was carried on, as Sakya owned a large trove of Buddist texts; all that were left after India's libraries were burned down by Muslim invaders. A separate sect of Tibetan Budhism took from here, named Sa-Skya-Pa. Nothing remains of the first monastry today. It fell into disrepair by the 15th century and was demolished in recent times. High foundations built into the mountain side can only be seen.

Three buildings of the 13th century monastry remain, protected by massive windowless fortress walls with corner towers. The monastry is entered on the west side. It includes the main Hall, an East Hall and a Dormitory building with a five facade for Sakya's 30 Monks.

Guru Nanak visited this monastry in the ninth month of Tibetan Calender in 1516 AD. There is an interesting legend connected with Guru Nanak's visit to the place. The local people were much troubled by witches. The witches used to roast the flesh of human beings and disturbed the functions at Sakya Monastry. On the request of local lamas,

Guru Nanak is said to have cast spell on these witches and tied them turning them into masks. The local people were much pleased by this control of witches and started yearly celeberations on the day. On the day of the yearly celebrations these witchmasks are said to be shedding tears as they dance with chained body. The King of the area is stated to have presented Guru Nanak with costly robes. The blue and red robe is at present preserved at Lachin Monastry in North Sikkim.

Guru Nanak proceeded towards Sikkim from Sakya through Shigtse, Lawa Gompa and Chhorten Nyimala.

Guru's third entry into Tibet was just brief. After his travel to Sikkim, he entered Tibet's Chumbi valley from Ghora La and crossed Pharidzong on way to Bhutan.

He entered Tibet for the fourth time from Tawang (Arunachal Pradesh) and after crossing Nagu La and Tsangpo (Brahamputra). His route through Arunachal was through Lumla, Tawang, Zimithang Lumpung wherefrom he proceeded to Lhasa.

Lhasa

The city of Lhasa lies in the valley of Lhasa river, at an altitude of 3607 m (11830 ft). It is the capital of Tibet Antonomous Region and has been the seat of religious authority of Tibet since 7th century AD. The Jorkhang is the spiritual centre of Tibet, its most holy place, the destination over time, of million of Tibetan pilgrims. The oldest part of the Jorkhang dates from 7th century AD. It was one of the two temples built by King Songtsen Gampo to house the idols of Budha that his two foreign wives brought to Tibet from China and Nepal respectively.

Legend says that Songtsen Gampo threw his ring into the air, promising to build a temple wherever it landed. The ring fell into a lake and struck a rock where a white stupa miraculously appeared-an auspicious sign. Workmen filled in the lake with white stones and the Jorkhang was built over it by craftsmen from Tibet, China, Nepal and Kashmir. Even today, a pool exists under the Jorkhang's courtyard.

The Jorkhang temple was enlarged eight times between 7th century and 1660. It consists of an elaborate porch leading to a frescoed cloister around an open courtyard. Outside it rotates a long gallery of prayer wheels. A passage leads into a main hall with numerous small chapels around it. The sacred shrine holding the ancient Budha idol is centred at the rear of the main hall. Above, another floor has historically valuable murals.

The main hall is entered through a corridor guarded by guardian statues-fierce on the left, benign on the right. Here a delightful set of murals depicts Wen Chang's the queen from China procession coming to Tibet with the statue enthroned in a horse-drawn carriage, and then the building of the Jorkhang. In the middle of the hall sit two huge images of Padmasambhva (left) and Sakyamuni (right). Between them, a delicate eleven headed Chenrezi expresses infinite compassion.

Above, beams carved as human faced lions show Persian influence brought in via Kashmir. Guru Nanak visited Jorkhang monastry where he was offered refreshments, made comfortable and approached with a request for answers to certain questions, Guru answered these questions with great magnanimity.

Lamas asked, "There are many creeds prevalent in India and the learned expound many philosophies. What do you say about the creation of the world and the creator.[32]

Guru said, "From the soundless Absolute proceeds everything,
He the soundless emanates sound.
And from it flows forth air, water, fire, light and sound.
He, the Absolute remains unaffected and yet maintains for ever.
He, the Lord of creation, rejoices in His own creations,
The Absolute produces Brahma, Vishnu, Shiva,
And also time and the four great ages.
He who knows the Absolute as all pervading,
Is a perfect man, and in his company
Delusion is destroyed".

The Lama heaved a deep sigh, "I have heard the theory of Absolute and your definition has cleared it a good deal. Tell me more about it. Guru replied, "(*Hukmi Hovan Aakaar.* (Japuji Sahib)[33].

By Him are all forms created,
By Him infused with life and blessed,

By Him are some to excellence elated,
Others born lowly and depressed,
By His writ some have pleasure, others pain;
By His grace, some are saved,
Others doomed to die, relive and die again.
He will encompasses all, there by none besides.
O Nanak, He who knows, hat no ego and no pride.

"How can we reach the Absolute?" Asked the Lama.
The Guru Replied,

> "As a beggar goes abegging, bowl in one hand, staff in the other, rings in his ears, in ashes smothered, so go thou forth in life with ear-ings made of contentment, with modesty the begging bowl, dedication the fabric of your garment, knowledge of death the cowl. Let your mind be chaste virginal clean, Faith your staff on which to lean. You shall humiliate your fancy with mind subdue, the world subjugate."[34] (japuji Sahib).

The Lamas were very much satisfied and pleased.

At Lhasa, Guru Nanak was told about another famous monastry in South East Tibet. The monastry was known as Samye Monastry. The famous religious centre and the centre of teaching of Nying-Ma-Pa (Karma-pa) sect, the sect which became follower of Guru Nanak. The Guru proceeded towards Samye Monastry: enroute he halted near Cherisarma. There a cap shaped peak is worshipped by the local people. They go around this hill as if doing parikarma of Sri Harimandar Sahib. The cap shaped peak is believed to be the Seli Topi (cap) of Guru Nanak which the Guru left to protect the hill people therefrom demons.

From Cherisherma Guru Nanak proceeded towards Samye Monastry.

Samye

Samye monastry is Tibet's first monastry which is located north of the Yarlong (Tsangpo) river about 30 km from Tsedang in South-Eastern Tibet as the crow flies. To reach Samye, one has to stop at a ferry 36 km west of Tsedang and cross the river in an open, flat bottomed boat propelled by a converted tractor engine. The crossing may take an hour or more depending on the height of the water and position of sandbanks. The ferry lands serveral kilometers upstream from Samye. The remainder journey can be covered in a tractor drawn wagon over a rough desert track.

The monastry surrounded by a village, is in a green valley among barren mountains set back from the Jarlong Tsangpo. Haibur, its small holy mountain stands just to the east. Five ancient stupas perched on crags overlook an early part of the trail from the ferry to Samye.

Samye Monastry was founded in 770 by Trisong Detsen, Tibet's Second Religius King, after he invited prominent Buddhists to Tibet from India, the most famous of whom were Padmasambhva, the magician saint, and Santarakshita, his personal tutor. The two teachers helped him found Samye as a school to train Tibetan monks, modelling it after a monastry in Bihar. Legends say; Padmasambhva magically compelled Tibetan demons to haul stones and wood from river and forests each night so men could build the monastry by day, and forced the Nagas the water-serpent deities, to give up their gold to finance their operation. (It may be that the Nagas may be the people, who ruled this area before. They later settled in Nagaland).

The first Tibetan monk, who had attended a Buddist university in India was ordained and installed as first abbot. In 791, King Trisong Detsen proclaimed Buddhism the official religion i.e., Bon faith. A clash occured in which Chinese intervened and installed their own abbot. Chinese Chan Buddhism was being forced in, in place of lamaism.

A great debate took place in the king's presence from 792 to 793, Two learned monks one from China, the other from India, led the discussion. The Indian view triumphed and was adopted as the future course for Tibetan Budhism to follow.

It took over a decade, 775-787, to build Samye, at the site of a temple founded by Trisong Detsan's father. At the centre was a large three storeyed hall surmounted by gold roofs, enclosed inside a protective cloister with elaborate gates at the cardinal points. Opposite the corners stood four big stupas,

Built by individuals in different pegoda styles, coloured red, white, green and black. Many surrounding buildings and temples completed the monastry. The whole monastry was originally enclosed by a zigzag wall that was destroyed by fire. It was replaced in the tenth century by a great circular wall 12 ft (31/2m) high and 21/2 km (11/2) mile in circumference.

The architecture of the Great Hall combined styles that expressed the borrowing and merging typical of Tibetan Buddism. The lower part was constructed in the Tibetan manner with two roofs, by builders from Khotan. The middle part was made in Chinese style, with three roofs, by Chinese carpenters. The upper part, also with three roofs, was built in Indian style by Indian craftsmen.

All that remains today is the Great Hall without its third storey and roofs, and the surrounding cloister which houses 34 monks. The Great Hall faces east. The square cloister compound is entered by the east portal with its two stone-elephants and giant bronze bell; just inside is a huge prayer wheel under a canopy.

A major pilgrim path runs from Lhasa to Samye, a hard walking trip of four days and three nights, passing through maximum altitude of 4850m (16,000ft). The path starts from Dagze Dzong, 27 km east of Lhasa.

Guru Nanak visited this monastry in the year 1516 A.D and the followers of Guru projected their doubts which Guru Nanak cleared.

From Samyye monastry the Guru proceeded southwards towards India. Crossing through La-Khanya, he reached Menchukha a place where Lord Shiva one of the Hindu Trinty is said to have meditated. Guru Nanak was enchanted by the place and stayed for sometime and meditated. He went back to Tibet and brought his followers of Memba sect from Dakbo-Kongba area and got them settled in Menchukha valley. Therefrom, through Tibet he proceeded towards Gelling-Tuting valley in March 1516.

Guru Nanak's next visit to Tibet is after his return from East Asia. Janamsakhi Bhai Bala states that Guru Nanak after visiting Silmila Dweep and Suwarnpur went to Sumer again[35]. Dr. Surender Singh Kohli wrote that 'it was about 1517 when Guru Nanak entered Kashmir from Sinkiang province of China. In China he is said to have gone as far as Nanking and was on his return journey[36]. An interview with Chhimed Ringdzin Rimpoche by this Researcher reveals that Guru Nanak came from China through North Tibet visiting the famous Kokonoor lake. The legend of Kokonoor lake is also attributed to Guru Nanak. Guru Nanak after visiting North Eastern Tibet, again visited Lhasa and Mansarovar and through Gortok (Garu), Rudok and Panjong lake area entered Ladakh via Chushul[37].

References

1. Binoy Roy Burman : *Religion and Politics in Tibet*, Vikas Publishing House, New Delhi, P-344.
2. Author's Article : *Tibet and India-Ancient Links*, Sainik SAmachar, July 1988.
3. S. C. Dass : *Contribution on the Religion and History of Tibet*, New Delhi, 1970, P-35.
4. Shakabpa W.B. : *Tibet*: A Political History, London, 1976, P.60.
5. Bell Charles : *Tibet*: Past and present ; Oxford, 1924, P.32
6. Ibid
7. Ibid
8. Mac-Donald, David : *The Land of the Lama*, London, 1929:
9. *Puratan Janam Sakhi* (ed. Shamsher Singh Ashok), P-96
10. Dalvinder Singh Grewel (Colonel) : *Guru Nanak's travels to Himalayan region.*
11. *Bhai Gurdas* : Varan : SGPC Amritsar, 1964, P-14.
12. *Sri Guru Granth Sahib* : P-938-946.
13. *Puratain Janamsakhi*, P-97.
14. *Sri Guru Granth Sahib*, P981.
15. *Ibid*, P-458.
16. *Puratan Janamsakhi*, P-97.
17. *Ibid*, P-97.
18. *Sri Guru Granth Sahib*, P-468.
19. *Puratan Janamsakhi*, P-97.
20. *Sri Guru Granth Sahib*, P-145.
21. *Bhai Gurdas* : Varan : (1/31) P-16.
22. *Puratan Janamsakhi*, P-98.
23. *Ibid*, P-100.
24. *Sri Guru Granth Sahib*, P-359.
25. *Puratan Janamsakhi*, P-101.
26. *Sri Guru Granth Sahib*, P-360.
27. *Puratan Janamsakhi* P-103.
28. Varma Sharad Chander : *Guru Nanak* P-217.
29. Verma Sharad Chandra. *Guru Nanak* P215.
30. Kirpal Singh (Dr.) (Ed) ; *Janam Sakhi Prampara* : P-106.
31. Daljit Singh (Raja, Sir) : *Guru Nanak* : Lahore Book Shop, 1979:
32. *Sri Guru Granth Sahib*, P-1.
33. *Ibid*, P-6.
34. *Janamsakhi Bhai Bala* ed. by Kirpal Singh P-280.
35. Surender Singh Kohli (Dr), P-128.
36. Fauja Singh Kirpal Singh *'Atles Travels of Guru Nanak's* P-63.

Nepal

Nepal, spreading over a length of 800 Kms and a breadth of 150-200 Km, is diagonally cut by the 28 degress latitude south of the Himalayan main ridge, the eastern part of which also forms the northern frontier with Tibet. The Nepalese territory crosses over the central Himalaya at some places in the west, specially in the region of Mustang and extends till the Tibetan plateau. In the South, Nepal borders the Indian states of Uttar Pradesh, Bihar and West Bengal and in the east, the Sikkim. Climatewise the region can be divided roughly into three regions, temparate and humid jungle infested; southern parts along Terai and Gangetic regions of India, the moderately cold regions which contain most of the middle ranges i.e. Siwalik and the Mahabharat chains with heights ranging between 2000-3000m, (valleys like Kathmandu and Pokhara lie in this region) and extremely cold region around Himalayan Peaks which include worlds' highest mountain Everest and other peaks like Dhaulgiri, Annapurna, Kanchanjanga, Gauri Shanker, Makalu etc. Many rivers flow in North-South direction through Nepal. The most important ones are the Seti, Karnali, Bhari, Kali-Gandaki, Buri-Gandaki, Trisuli, Sunkosi, Dudh-Kosi, Arun and Timur. Most of the old tracks were along these rivers only. Nepalese are deeply religious people. Though Nepal gave birth to Buddhism, yet it is the only country in the world which has Hinduism as its state religion. The deep religiousity of the Nepalese people finds expression in its multitudes of shrines and temples - over 6000 in Kathmandu alone.

The Nepal can also be called as one of the world's oldest monarchy surviving till today. Newars who settled down in Kathmandu Valley between 1000 and 700 BC have been dominating the Kathmandu Valley, the limb centre of entire Nepal. Lichhavis (400-750AD), Thakurs (750-1200AD), Mallas (1200-1768AD) and Gurkhas from 1768 AD have been the ruling dynasties. During Guru Nanak's period, Mallas of later period were the ruling dynasty. Yakshmalla, who ruled the state from 1462 to 1482 was a strong Malla king, but after his death the empire was split into smaller kingdoms under his heirs in 1482[1]. The kingdom was in a state of turmoil when Guru Nanak travelled this region.

Guru Nanak travelled in Nepal during his Sumer Udasi. He returned from Mansarover all along Kali Nadi which flows along the western border of Nepal. Thereafter, through Terai region, he entered Nepal. He also entered Nepal from Bihar. At Sitamarhi, where the famous temple of Sita stands he would have planned to go to Janakpur, the birth place of Sita. From Janakpur he is stated to have entered Birat Nagar and visited Chatra, situated on Sankosi/Kaushiki Nadi. I was told of a bunyan tree near Chatra, closer to the Dam site under which a small temple exists in the memory of Guru Nanak and is presently manned by an Udasi. This area is known as Varahkshetra or Koka-Mukh in old records. The Sikh Sangat of Siliguri specially those who have been visiting the site, were very eager to construct a Gurudwara at the site, but due to some legal problems the site could not be acquired and we could not progress much in this regard.

From Chatra, Guru Nanak visited the fort of Dhomri. From Dhomri he went through Shivpur, to Brahamkund where he attended a fair and delivered discourses to the people gathered over there. The people worshipped Yakshas. The Guru advised them to worship one God. He is remembered as Nanak Rishi in this Area.

After Brahamakund, Guru Nanak visited Lakhanpur and Palti lake. Therefrom, through the hills of Hawal Khanchi, he reached Krishna Tal area and preached True Name. After Krishna Tal, he proceeded through Dhaulgiri ridges to Belagarh and reached Kathmandu and Bhakatpur area, the two capitals of Patan and Banepa, the later Malla kings.

At Kathmandu, the Guru stayed near Pashupatinath temple on the bank of Baghmati Ganga. Here he preached the people not to do idol worship and made them devotees of the Lord. The King of Nepal, Raja asodhia Rajput Mahan Ranbir Singh came to the Guru and heard him intently. It is also stated that the king was blessed with two sons by Guru Nanak. There are two Dharamsalas in the memory of the Guru, one managed by Nirmalas and the other by Udasis. The Gurdwara is situated on a hill on the western bank of river Bishnumati. Buses are being organised by a Delhi Transport Company which go every year from Rakab Ganj/Gurdwara Bangla Sahib, New Delhi for the darshan.

In Kathmandu and around, Guru Nanak stayed for some weeks and visited the three capital areas, holding discussions with people of all walks of life. Kathmandu was known as Kantipur at the time of Guru Nanak's visit but given the name of Kathmandu later due to wood (Kath) temple platform (Mandu of Gorakhnath). The temple has been made out of the wood of one single tree. Other important temples in Kathmandu are Swami Shiv Nath temple, Bodhwati and Pashupatinath temples. Swami Shiv Nath temple is about two thousand years old, on a hillock which is reached by climbing 400 steps. It has a huge idol of Mahatma Buddha. Pashupatinath temple situated on the bank of river Baghmati is considered as the most sacred temple among Hindus. Lalitpur and Bhadgaon are the other important towns of Kathmandu Valley. Lalitpur, also known as Patan, is 5 Kms away from Kathmandu on the other side of Baghmati. Indian King Ashoka ordered construction of 5 stupas in this area. It was the capital town of Nepal at the time of Guru Nanak's visit. The Avalokiteshwara monastry built in 13th century, is one of the oldest monuments. Other temples of the period are the three stepped pagodas of the Red Machendranath and Kumbeshwar. Many other temples came up only in 17th & 18th century. Bhadgaon, also known as Bhaktapur (city of faithful) lies approximetely 16 km east of Kathmandu on the trade route to Tibet. It is the third royal city in Kathmandu Valley which during the period of Guru Nanak's visit was an independent kingdom. Amongst the old temples, is Changu Narayan, Pashupatinath or Vakshevar's temple dedicated to Shiva and Krishna. Temple was originally dedicated to Vishnu. Vatsada and Siddhilakshmi. The Buddhist monastry Chetur Varna Mahavihar was founded during the period of Guru Nanak's travels. Other temples were built later.

Guru Nanak visited most of these temples during his stay before he proceeded towards Tibet. From Kathmandu, Guru Nanak alongwith his companions is stated to have visited Thyangboche where his idol and a munuscript had been preserved. Guru Nanak is likely to have proceeded through Doleghat, Chiyaubas, Surke, Kiranti, Chap, Namdo, Kabra, Valleys of Jarsakhola and Sikri Khola, Jiri, Batasha Danda Ridge, Those, Shivalaya to Jhoding monastry at Thodungla and reached Bhander. From Bhander he is likely to have proceeded through Sate, Lamjurala. Sherpa villages of Dradobuk and Junbesi and visited Chiwang monastry. From Junsebi, he would have proceeded further through Phalali to Jubing, Kharela, Phakding and to Namche Bazar. From Namche Bazar, his next visit was to Khumjing monastry and Thayangboche. Thyangboche monastry situated at 3867 m. in the lap of Amba Dablam (6856m), is one of the most beautiful sites of the world on a table land, amidst breath taking scenery, surrounded by the Panorma of Khumbu - Himalaya with Mount Everest.[2] The 'Head Lama' of the Thyangbhoche monastry is a reincarnation, highly reverred by Sherpas. The scalp of a yeti, a snow ghost is kept and displayed in the monastry. Guru Nanak held discussions with the 'Head Lama' of the Thyangboche Monastry.

The Lamas were highly impressed by Guru's teachings and became the followers of Guru Nanak. A large sized idol of Guru Nanak and a manuscript of Guru Nanak were mentioned to be at the monastry by the famous Everst leader M.S. Kohli who writes, "The cupboards in Gompha contained many manustripts. There were idols of past lamas. These included an idol of Guru Nanak, Guru Rimphoce, Tibetans call Guru Nanak Guru Ramphoche".[3] His Holiness, the Head Lama told him that some writings of great Guru were in his personal possession.[4] From Thyangboche, Guru Nanak came back to Khumjing on the trading route of India- Tibet and proceeded to Tibet through Nanak La pass (5500m) (same name appears in the maps) and reached Tingri Dzong in Tibet. From Southern Tibet, he went to Sikkim through this route.

I planned to visit Thayangboche monastry but to my dismay; news appeared of this monastry getting electric short circuited and burnt with all its valuables including the manuscripts. With this my desire to get the sample of hand writings of Guru Nanak remained unfulfilled.

References

1. Manfred Gerner and Ahluwalia H.P.S. (Major) : *Himalaya*, P-289 to 334.
2. Ibid, P- 318-352.
3. Surinder Singh Kohli (Dr.), *Travels of Guru Nanak*, P-116.
4. ibid

GURU NANAK IN SIKKIM

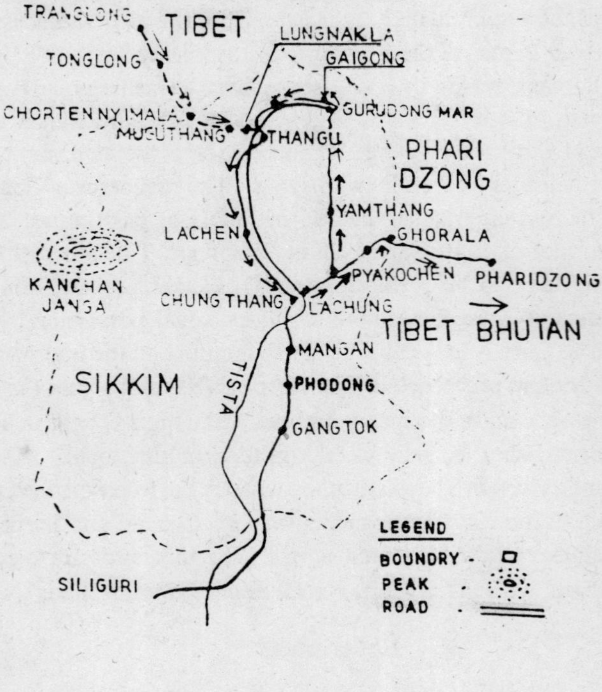

ROUTE ADOPTED BY GURUNANAK
THROUGH SIKKIM, NEPAL, ARUNACHAL & ASSAM STATES

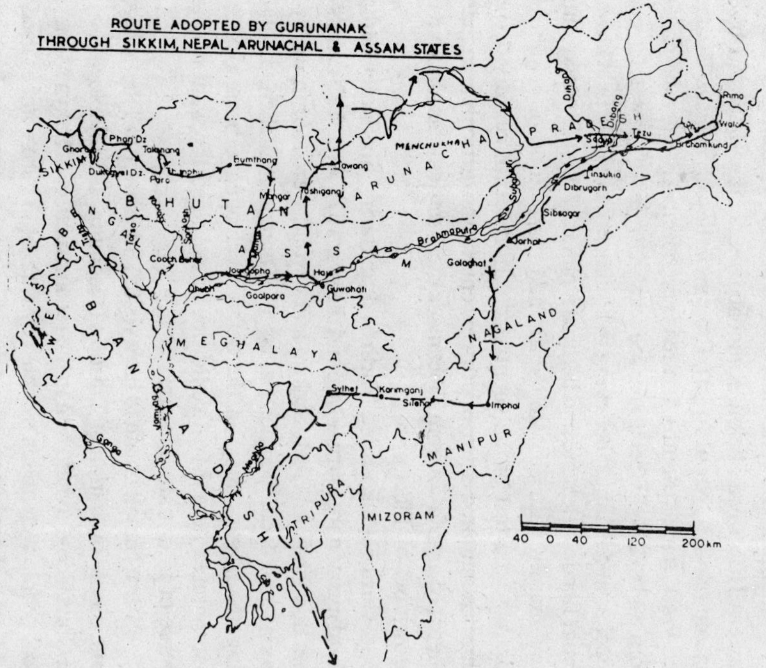

Sikkim

Sikkim is the 22nd state of Indian Union perched in the lap of the Eastern Himalayas, below Kanchandzonga. It is bounded by Tibetan plateau (North), Nepal (west), Chumbi valley of Tibet & Bhutan (East) and West Bengal (South). Its area is predominatly hilly, heights ranging from 800 to 28000 feet above see level. Originally, it was the country of Lepchas and Bhutias (believing in Lamaism), but later the Gurkhas from Nepal flooded the state and became a majority. Lepchas and Bhutias are now mainly restricted to North and East Sikkim, while Nepalese dominate the rest of the countryside. In fifteenth century, Lepcha and Bhutia dominated entire Sikkim except the the difficult area in the north where Nying-Ma-Pa from Tibet made their settlements after having been thrown out of Tibet.

Guru Nanak visited North Sikkim during his Sumer Parbat Udasi (third missionary journey) around the year 1516 A.D. The details of Guru Nanak's visits to Tibet, Sikkim and beyond were told to me by various Lamas and local people. Lamas of Thanggu, Lachen, Lachung and Muguthang gave most of the details which have been examined and incorporated here. Myth could not be excluded for want of alternative source of information to counter it.

Guru Nanak is said to have visited Sikkim from Tibet where he had gone on the invitation of Trasung Deochung, the then local Nying-Ma-Pa Chief/King, to help him in the reconstruction of Sakya Monastry. The local people were much troubled by witches. These witches used to roast the flesh of human beings and disturb the reconstruction/functions at the monastry. Guru Nanak is said to have reached this place in the ninth month of Tibetan Calendar. When he is stated to have tied the witches and turned them into masks. On the day of the annual celebrations of this monastry these witchmasks are stated to be shedding tears and dance chained. Guru Nanak was presented a robe by the Local Chief/King which is now preserved in Lachen Monastry. This writer examined it at Lachen.

From Tibet, Guru entered Sikkim through Chorten-Nyimala. Near Chorten Nyimala, there are 108 small lakes commemmorating Guru's visit. Seeing the natural beauty of the area, Guru Nanak got in ecstacy and broke his rosary. The 108 beads spread around and are stated to have formed lakes. This added to the beauty of the area further.

After cossing Chorten Nyimala pass, Guru Nanak came to Dolma Sampa and Tongpen enroute to Muguthang. He also visited Kedang, Bendu, Sherang, Lyingka, and number of other hutments sprung up during the upsurge of Nying-Ma-Pa and Kar-Ma-Pa sect from Tibet.

In Muguthang valley, there is a lake which, according to a local legend had demons who used to swallow human beings. Local people requested Guru Nanak for protection. Guru Nanak picked up a huge boulder and threw it towards the lake. The lake-devils', a male and a female, sensing the danger, came out of the lake and requested for forgiveness. Guru Nanak forgave them and held the falling stone with rope. The same stone can still be seen hanging over the lake. The rope marks too are visible. These two devils were forbidden eating human flesh and were redeemed by guiding them to True Name, the Name of God. An annual local fair honouring Guru's visit is held at the place since then. Guru Nanak, thereafter, visited Kedang, Sherang and Gulang valleys. At Kedang, he was enchanted by the beauty of the green lush valley. He blessed the valley as a happy and bewitching and called it 'ki dang' (which astonishes).

From, Muguthang Guru went to Lawu Gompha through Naku la where from he proceeded towards Guru Dongmar. In Gurudongmar lake area, the graziers approached Guru Nanak to solve their problem of water shortage as the lakes all around froze in winter due to low temperatures at that altitude (17500 feet). Guru Nanak hit the water with his stick. The ice melted giving way to milky water. Since then, the water of the lake is stated to have never frozen. The lake and the hill feature atop came to be known as the Gurudongmar lake and hill respectively. This writer found these names in the maps printed in nineteenth century. The water of the lake has been found unaffected even in December-January, when the snow fall rises to 10 feet and the temperature falls to 30 degree minus.

Some graziers projected another problem to Guru Nanak. Due to the effect of altitude, their virility was effected. They requested him to do something about it. Guru Nanak blessed the Gurudongmar lake saying "whoever takes the water of this lake will gain virility and strength". The people of the area have firm faith in Guru's words and the water of the lake is considered as nectar by the people.

This lake is the source for Teesta River flowing through Sikkim, & Bengal. A Gurudwara has now been constructed at the site and Sri Guru Granth Sahib is placed; though the service of a regular priest could not be obtained despite my best efforts. This was because of extreme cold conditions there. The 800 X 500 yards lake became a place of great attraction soon after my earlier articles on this subject. A helipad had been constructed and a well-constructed road leads upto the Gurudwara and lake site.

From Gurudongmar, Guru Nanak came to Thanggu. At Thanggu, he relaxed under a boulder stone. The people having heard about his miracles already, thronged to him. He blessed the devotees and delivered sermons. His foot marks were stated to be existent on a huge boulder by the side of Teesta river but the ignorant road construction party blew off the boulder stone in 1987. The stone fell into the river and was recovered by Lachen Lama and preserved in Lachen Monastry. At Thanggu in Guru's memory a Gompa and a Chorten were erected in which 1002 idols of Guru Nanak are preserved. A Gurdwara has been constructed in the Engineer Company area to commemmorate Guru Nanak's visit to the place. His next stay was at Lachen, In Lachen Gompha, Guru Nanak's foot marks on a stone are preserved. Also a dress given to him by the then Tibetan king is also preserved. From Lachen he proceeded towards south and relaxed near Munsithang where he found a hot water spring. His body marks are stated to be existing near this location.

From Munshithang, Guru Nanak moved to South Chungthang (height 6000 feet). Local people call Chungthang as Nanakthang. Here, Guru Nanak spent his a few nights, after his visit to Gurudongmar. There is a boulder stone 30 feet in diameter and 20 feet high commommerating Guru Nanak's visit. As Guru Nanak relaxed near a boulder a devil staying on nearby hill, threw a heavy stone on Guru Nanak. The boulder was brought to a halt by Guru Nanak with a stick. He then climbed on to the stone to warn the demon Having seen Guru Nanak unruffled the demon fell at his feet. Guru Nanak asked him not to disturb the local people to leave the place and to follow the True Name of Lord, which all he finally did. Foot prints indicating Guru Nanak's climbing atop the stone are reminiscent of the event. The stick with which he diverted the stone was stuck into the earth in a straight posture. This stick has now taken the form of a tree, and is known as 'Babe di Khoondi'.

Sitting at the top of the stone, Guru Nanak opened his lunch pack consisting of rice packed in banana leaves. The local people had not seen banana leaves or rice earlier. They prayed "We dont have paddy and banana in our area. Please favour us with these". Guru Nanak threw some left-over rice around the boulder and burried the banana leaves. He then announced, "Henceforth paddy and bananas shall always be grown in this valley". Chungthang has been the only place in the area for long around where paddy and bananas grew, since Guru's visit.

A woman living in a nearby hut requested, "I have to bring water from a distance. I am old. Moving down and climbing up is very difficult for me. Pray, do something about it". Guru Nanak scratched one side of the boulder with his hands and there appeared a spring. This spring (Chashma) on the side of the boulder has been flowing ever since. The blessings bestowed upon these people by Guru Nanak are known to be the cause of prosperity of Chungthang valley. The local people always remember him and worship him with great devotion.

They also say that Guru Nanak's sacred scripture and one tourlice were left under the boulder stone, which will be taken out by Guru Nanak's successor at an appropriate occasion in this century.

The local lamas worship Guru Nanak as Nanak Lama. They built a Gompha (Lama temple) commemmorating his visit. In the Gompha, a lamp of pure ghee burns day and night to enliven the memory of the visit.

An Assam Rifles Batallion stationed at Chungthang constructed an impressive building of Gurudwara under the guidance of Subedar Major Bhullar. The Gurudwara is now called Gurudwara Nanak Lama. The Local M.L.A. takes keen interest in the protection, maintenance and upliftment of the place. 'Babe di khoondi" is now a shapely tree which attracts the visitors and the worshippers alike. The foot prints are well preserved. The water from the spring is considered as a source of strength and sign of purity and is being taken as charanamrit. The rice field is bounded by a wall and well secured. The saffren (kesri) flag can be seen from miles and no effort is needed to find the place as it is now in the centre of the valley as well as the town.

From Chungthang, Guru nanak is stated to have proceeded to Phodong. A grand monastry is the reminiscent of Guru Nanak's visit. The head of the monastry is considered as the reincarnation of Guru Nanak and an organised succession system exists. The present successor of Nanak Lama was installed in 1989. The installation ceremony appeared in the columns of local papers with photographs.

From Phodong, Guru Nanak returned to Chungthang and went to Lachung (height 9500 ft). In Lachung monastry at the top of a nearby hill, there were excellent wall-paintings depicting Guru Nanak's visit to the area which now stand obliterated. After Leachung, Guru is stated to have stayed at Yumthang enroute to Tibet and Bhutan. At Yumthang, Guru Nanak found these people rather unclean. They did not take bath for months as the water of the area was cold. Guru Nanak displaced a stone and a hot spring appeared. The gushing water formed a rivulet. Guru Nanak asked the local people to have regular bath and worship The God in the morning. The people follow Guru's teachings till now. From Yumthang, Guru Nanak proceeded to Phari Dzong through Pyakochin and Ghorala. At Pyakochim a writing in Gurmukhi cameorates Guru's visit. Yumthang was developed into a place of tourist attraction and the Sikkim National Transport organises visits to Chungthang, Lachung and Yumthang. Buses ply regularly from[1] Gangtok to Chungthang. Gangtok is approachable from Siliguri - New Jalpaiguri - Bagdogra complex. Distance and time wise Siliguri to Gangtok is about 95 Kms (4 hours by bus), Gangtok to Phodong 35 kms (1 hour by bus), Gangtok to Chungthang 95 kms (3½ hours by bus), Chungthang to Lachung 40 kms (1 hour by bus). Chungthang to Yumthang 60 kms (2 hours by bus). For going to Lachen, Thanggu and Gurudongmar, a different route has to be adopted from Chungthang. By road, Lachen is about 1 hour from Chungthang and another hour upto Thanggu. From Thanggu it takes about 2 hours upto Gurudongmar, the road however has been built upto Giagong recently and a track leads thereafter. For going beyond Chungthang, a security clearance is required to be obtained from Sikkim

Government and Army authorities. This clearance can be obtained or pre-arranged at Gangtok, the state capital of Sikkim.

To reach Gangtok, the rail head and air-port are New Jalpaiguri/ Siliguri/Bagdogra (all within 20 kms to each other). From Siliguri, Sikkim National Transport runs half an hour service to Gangtok. New Jalpaiguri/Siliguri are connected by rail direct to Delhi/Calcutta/Patna and Bagdogra is connected to Delhi/Calcutta/Guwahati by air. There are numerous hotels as well as Government rest houses at Siliguri and Gangtok and a few at Chungthang.

Places In Sikkim connected with Guru Nanak's Travels

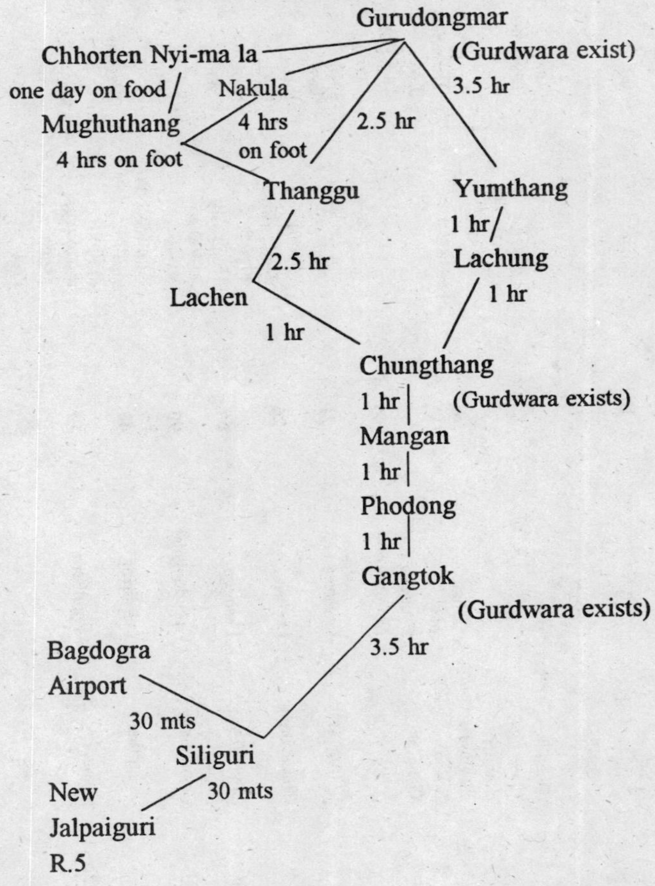

Draft

Places in Sikkim Connected With Guru Nanak

Dist & Tims Chart

S.No.	From	To	Dist KM One Way	Terrain	Mode	Time One Way	Remarks
1.	Delhi	1. Siliguri 2. New Jalpai-guri 3. Bagdogra	1628	plain " "	Train "	22hrs 18	Meter gauge Broad gauge
2.	Bagdogra	Siliguri	23	"	Air	2hrs	
3.	New Jal-paiguri	-do-	22	"	Taxi/Bus "	30mts "	
4.	Bagdogra	Gangtok	98	Hilly	Helicopter	30 mts	on availability
5.	Siliguri	-do-	98	"	Taxi	3½ hrs	
6.	Gangtok	Phodong	37	"	Taxi/Bus	1 hr	
7.	Gangtok	Chungthang	99	"	Taxi	3½ hrs	
8.	Chungthang	Lachung	21	High Alti (9500)	Bus Taxi	5 hrs 1 hr	
9.	Chungthang	Lachen	26	High, Alti (7500)	Bus Taxi	2 hrs 1 hr	
10.	Chungthang	Thanggu	66	Hugh Alti v12000	Bus Taxi	1½ hrs 3 hrs	
11.	Changthang	Gurudongmar	90	Super. Altitude 17000	Taxi	5hrs	
12.	Chungthang	Yumthang	45	Alti (13000)	Taxi/bus	2hrs	
13.	Thanggu -	Muguthang	20	Super Alti 15000 Feet	Man Pack mule	5 hrs	

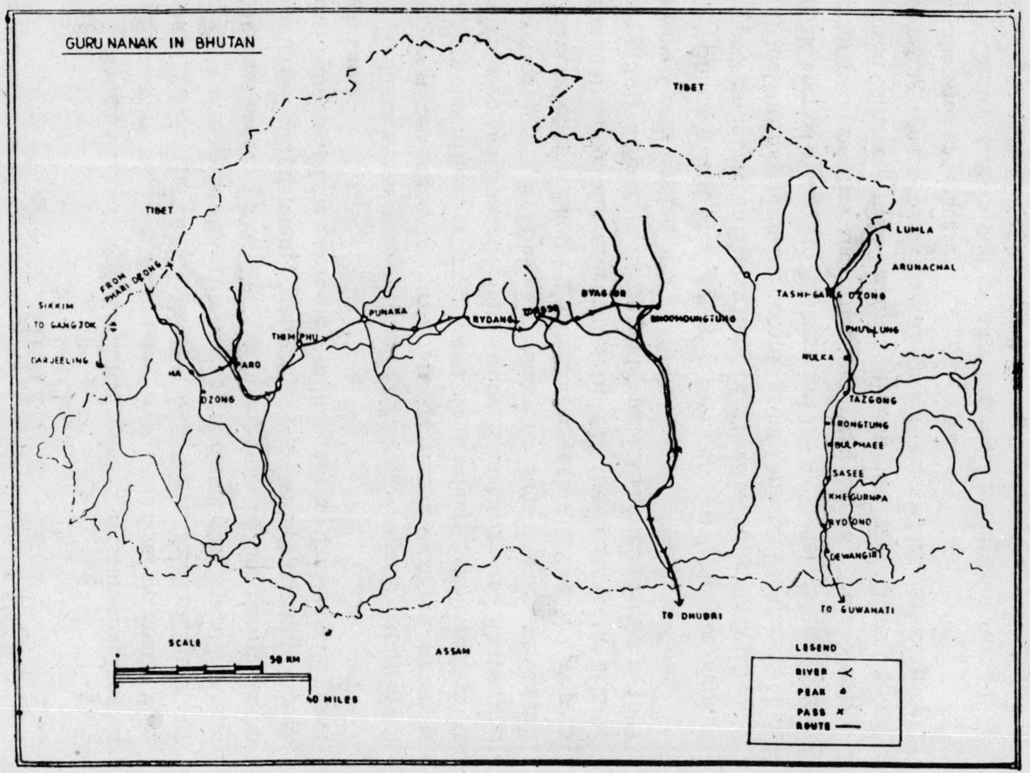

GURU NANAK IN BHUTAN

Bhutan

Bhutan is a land locked country, bounded by Arunachal Pradesh and Assam in thc East, Assam and West Bengal in the South, West Bengal, Sikkim and Tibet in the West and Tibet in the North. Its 18,000 Sq Miles territory nestles in the heart of the Himalayas. Some 144.84 km (90 miles) wide and 305.7 km (190 miles) long, the kingdom of Bhutan is unforgettable mountain-country bejewelled with picturesque shrines, forts, hamlets and monastries and rolling valleys guarded by ranges of mountains.

Bhutan is now ruled by King Jigme Dorji Wangchuck, third in the dynasty succeeding to the throne. The ancient history of this country is not very clear. However, major event of 8th century is well marked. As Indian sage and Buddhist Saint Padma-Sambhav visited Bhutan and converted the people of Bhutan to Buddhism, Buddhism became and still is the state religion. Bhutan's historical records are believed to have been burnt in fire, flood and earth quakes. In 1827, fire burnt over the historic dzong (fort) in Punakha, the ancient capital, and an earthquake in 1897 destroyed what was left of it.

Bhutan's first king whose records are available was Drukpa Rimpoche who came to Bhutan from Tibet in 1616. So far not much could be found out from historical records about Guru Nana's travels. Guru Nanak's period of travel to Bhutan is in 1516 A.D. after Sikkim. By then the larger monastries and dzong had been founded. Guru Nanak is believed to have visited Tashi-Cho-Dzong monastry. There are very interesting legends connected with the holy Guru which the local people describe with reverence.

Guru Nanak is said to have entered Bhutan from North-East Bhutan after his visit to Sikkim and Chumbi valley. From Pharidzong in Chumbi valley, he entered Paro valley, and visited the Dukhgyel Dzong, the Eastern fort of Bhutan, famous for its great round towers. Taksang (the Tiger's Den) was the next place he visited. Haw and Paro monastries were also visited by him. This monastry is a valuable treasure of art and religious paintings and books. Guru's painting is also said to be preserved there. The holy Guru is believed to have tamed the dreaded domons and tigers of the area. Tiger's Den is stated to be the reminiscent of the same event.

The story of Tiger's Den monastry as recorded in Sikh chronicles goes as follows; "At one place in that region there wwere millions of lions. The Guru asked his companion Mardana to play upon the rebec. On hearing the sweet music, the hearts of lions were softened and they came near the Guru. The Guru asked them, "How have you come here?" They replied, "On seeing you we have gained the power of speech. Our previous sins had brought us in this form. We have a feeling that you have come to us as a redeemer". The Guru asked them again, "On what food you live?". They replied, "We have eaten up all the animals of this forest which is spread over one hundred yojnas. If anyone now amongst us feels drowsy, he is immediately eaten up by others, therefore we always stand without sleep. We beseech you to get our release from this state". The Guru said, "You will become human beings in your next birth but you will get the final emancipation only on following the instructions of the perceptor". The Guru left the forest and came to the town and the people wondered how he and his companions escaped death because the lions were very fierce and they spared none. They said, "We have built this town on the tip of the mountain and have kept the cannons on all the points leading to the town for the fear of these lions. We do not understand how you have not been devoured by them". The Guru said "I have made them non-violent. All of them will die after some time for want of food". All the inhabitants of the town felt very much pleased and became disciples of the Great Guru"[1]

From Paro, Guru Nanak visited Thimpu and Tashi-Cho-Dzong. Over looking Tashi-Cho-Dzong is the 'white Glacier of the three Spiritual Brothers'. This is said to be in reminiscence of the visit of Guru Nanak and his two disciples.[2]

At Tashi-Cho-Dzong, Guru Nanak visited the chief monastry. The Head Lama of the monastry benefitted from his company and translated several hymns of the Guru in Bhutia language. He also visited the residence of the Dharamraja and held discussions with him. The details of discussions as recorded in Janamsakhi B 40 are as follows:-

"Story of Bhutant Desh starts : Nanak Baba came to Bhutan Country. He came and sat in a garden. Whoever came to pay him obeissance, stayed there itself; neither he could get up nor could go home. People around started discussing about this. They talked about Guru Nanak, stating, 'A great man has come to this country who neither eats nor drinks anything nor speaks to anyone. Neither he begs nor he takes any offering from anyone; he sans all desire'; The king of the area heard of this and came to him (Guru Nanak). He brought choicest dresses and eatables, and fell at his feet (Guru Nanak). By then Baba (Guru Nanak) had watched the system of the functioning of the state. The king used to grow grass. He wore fur dress. However a girl from his kingdom married, instead of going to her husband for the first night she had to be sent to the king. Baba Nanak told the king, "O King! Whatever evils you are doing, you must leave. This is the order of the Guru. Whatever you wish you must ask from me. Guru (Nanak) is in a mood to bless you". The king then said, "O Baba, rice and wool are in abundance in my country but nothing else grows". Guru Nanak blessed the country with all types of mines, fragrances and cloth. The mines included those of gold, silver, zinc and lead. Many products like musk, silk and fruit started growing in those mountains. The king alongwith his people then became the disciple of Guru Nanak. Baba taught them True Name; to give alms to the poor and to have regular bath. A temple (Dharamsala) was established on the name of Guru Nanak. Guru then planned to move from the place. The king and the public came to request the Guru to stay. 'This country has been blessed by your arrival. You must stay here itself'. Baba saw that these people would not leave him like that. Sitting amongst them, he dived into the air and went to another country. Those sitting at the place were astonished. They exclaimed; Guru sitting with us a shortwhile before is seen nowhere. What unnatural event has happened! He has vanished ! It must be some miracle. We have not enjoyed his company to our heartfill. He was a great worshipper of God; very close to Him, but we could not identify such a saviour and helper of mankind". They were repentent of this, but Baba had gone. They started their daily life by regular prayers of the True Lord, giving alms to the poor, having regular baths and living truthfully"[3]

The holy Guru is said to have then visited Bumthang. The legend of "Hidden Treasure of Bumthang" is said to be connected with Guru Nanak. Legend goes like this. 'Pamlingpa, a dwarf like blacksmith and resident of Kunzamgda, when reached the age of twenty seven, went to the forest to look for mushrooms, but found none. On his way back, he met a hermit with a long white beard said to be Guru or 'Rimpoche' Nanak. Pamlingpa spoke to him full of respect, sadly mentioning that he had not found a single mushroom. The Guru smiled, bowed and with his hands pushed aside the twigs that were spread on the ground, revealing a whole bed of wonderful mushrooms. Pamlingpa collected them and invited the old man to the meals. Guru Nanak gave him a paper roll to preserve.

When they arrived at Pamlingpa's hut, the Guru stayed in the adjoining room and Pamlingpa cooked the mushrooms with five kinds of fragrant herbs. When they were ready, he went to call him in. But the Guru was no longer there; he seemed to have disappeared. Pamlingpa called him again and searched everywhere in vain. Finally and sadly, he ate the mushrooms alone. Afterwards he climbed the roof of his hut, lay down and musingly watched the clouds sweeping over the sky. Then he remembered that the hermit had given him a small paper roll, which he took from his packet and studied ponderingly. He had not learned to read, but intuitively he grasped the deeper meaning of the written message or it had been whispered into his ear. 'Go to the burning lake. There you will find a hidden treasure'. The massage was written in the so called 'fairy script' derived from Devnagri script of the Gods (probably Gurmukhi) which only a few could read. Pamlingpa understood more with his heart than with his mind, and it began to dawn on him that the event might have been a manifestation of Guru Rimpoche, who himself showed in this form in order to receive Pamlingpa as his true follower. Thus, according to the legend, Pamlingpa realised that he was in fact the embodiment of the true Guru. The legend goes on to describe how Pamlingpa got the spiritual treasure from the lake. This portion of the legend is akin to the legand connected with Guru Nanak's attainment of enlightsnment in Wein river.

'From Tashi-Cho-Dzong and Bumthang, Guru Nanak is said to

have visited Cental Bhutan where tell-tale indications are available of his visit. He is also said to have visited Askord where Guru Nanak's paintings are preserved'[4].

From Bhutan Guru Nanak travelled to North Bengal, and to Dhubri via Cooch Behar. From Dhubri, through Guwahati and Hajo, Guru Nanak again entered Bhutan along the Manas river and enroute to Tawang (in Arunachal) and Lhasa (Tibet) visited Mongar and Tashi-Gongdzong in East Bhutan. From Tashi-Gongdzong, Guru Nanak went along Tawang Chu and reached Lumla in Tawang District of Arunachal Pradesh.

To visit the places connected with Guru Nanak's travels to Bhutan, one has to obtain the visa to Bhutan at Delhi and then reach Siliguri/New Jalpaiguri (West Bangal) by train or to Calcutta or Bagdogra by air. Bhutan Government buses are available at Siliguri and also at Calcutta which take you to Phuntsoling, the border check post at Indo-Bhutan border. These buses further take the travellers to Thimpu, the capital of Bhutan, where good hotels exist for food and lodging. For going to Tashi-Gongdzong, buses are available from Guwahati. Guwahati is connected by rail, road and air to Delhi. The journey into Bhutan is hilly and climate is cold to very cold from summer to winter.

References

1. Surinder Singh Kohli : 1969 (1978 Reprint) : *Travels of Guru Nanak,* Chandigarh, Punjab University, P.174-5.
2. Statement by cept Bikkas Singh posted in Hawe Indian Miltary Team.
3. Piar Singh, Dr., 1974 (Reprint 1989). *Janamsakhi Sri Guru Nanak Dev ji*, B40. P.124-5
4. Lal Singh Giani : 1940 (Reprint 1955). *Guru Khalsa Twarikh,* Ludhiana, Lahore Book Shop, P-36

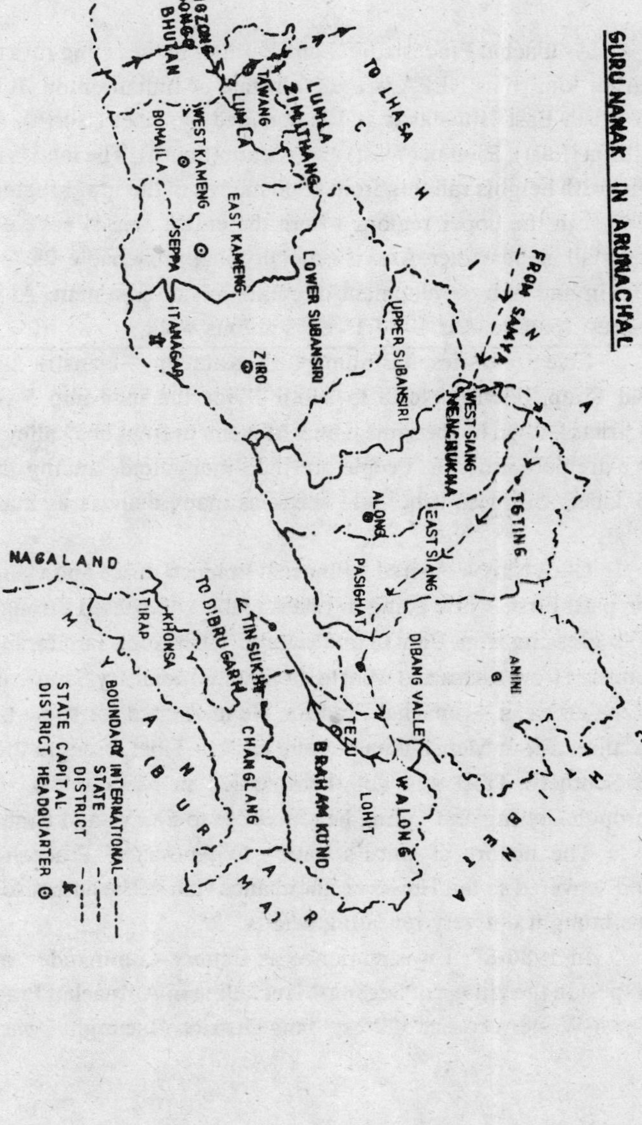

GURU NANAK IN ARUNACHAL

Arunachal Pradesh

Arunachal Pradesh the 'Land bathing in the rising rays of the sun' earlier known as NEFA is the 26th state of Indian union. It is situated in North-East Himalayas and is bounded by Tibet (North), China and Burma (East), Bhutan (West) and Assam (South). The land is mountainous, with heights ranging from 1500 metres in the lower regions to 7000 metres in the upper regions where the entire area is covered by thick snowfall in the winter. Area is generally unapproachable due to its rugged terrain and non-development of communication system. At places the nearest road head is 10 to 15 days ardous walk.

Five tributaries of Brahmaputra, Kameng, Subansiri, Siang, Lohit and Tirap, flowing North to South divide the state into 5 valleys and districts known by the same name. Movement from one valley to another is extremely difficult. People are Indo-mongoloid, tracing their origin to Tibets-Burmese tribes and speak as many dialects as many are the tribes.

Guru Nanak entered Arunachal Pradesh thrice and visited most of the part. First, while going to Lhasa (Tibet) he passed through Tawang after crossing from Bhutan and entered Tibet from Samdurang Chu. He returned from Lhasa and went to the famous monastry Samya and entered Menchukha in Arunachal Pradesh. He meditated for some time at this location. From Menchukha he went back to Tibet, brought the residents of Southern Tibet and got them settled in Menchukha. Thereafter, through Gelling and Tuting he proceeded to Saidya and Braham-Kund.

The history of Guru's travels to Arunachal Pradesh had been undiscovered so far. However, the chance visit of the author to the places has brought out very revealing details.

In 1986-87, I was stationed as Battery Commander, at an army outpost in the village of Segang-Menchukha in Arunachal Pradesh in the North-Western corner of West Siang District. One night I was woken up in the middle of the night by loud and persistent knocking at my door. 'Who could it be'? I wondered.

When I opened the door, I found it to be the village headman, locally known as the Gaon Burha. He was in an obvious state of distress and told me that his son was dying of a very severe pain in his stomach and if I would send for a doctor. I thought that before I telephoned the doctor, who was some distance away and the track was quite hazardous, I had better ascertained the condition of the patient. So I decided to accompany the Gaon Burha. He led me to his wooden hut, which was divided into two; the portion in front was for cooking and at the rear was the living room, where I found a young boy writhing in pain and crying. As a precautionary measure, I had taken some pain-killing tablets with me, which I offered to the sick boy. A lama, standing nearby, told the boy not to take the medicine. It puzzled me but there was little I could do because the lamas are held in great esteem by these very superstitious people of the area.

However, immediately after, the lama started saying a prayer obviously in order to appease the evil spirits. He first fashioned an idol with rice and butter, lit some incense and, to the accompaniment of the ringing of a bell, started murmuring his prayers. After he had finished doing so, he took the incense to the bedside of the sick boy, read out 'Om Mani Padme Hum' to him and then asked him to take the medicine I had given.

The idol that the lama had made, aroused my curiosity. I therefore asked him as to whose idol was it that he worshipped. 'Guru Nanak', he said. I must say I was quite astonished with his answer because I never expected anyone in this area, nearly 2,000 kilometers away from the Punjab, would know anything about Guru Nanak much less worship his idol. I probed him for further details. He told me : "We worship Guru Nanak and consider him as one of our Guru Rimpoches, the sacred Guru. We call him Guru Nanak of Amritsar also. His idol is worshipped in our Gompa on Dorgilling Hill. It is said that the Guru visited this area and meditated in Pemoshubu. Pemoshubu lay about 5 kilometers away from where we were.

"During his meditation", continued the lama, "the Guru was attacked by a bear but the huge boulder, under which the Guru was meditating, lifted him up and took him in his lap, according to this legend. The bear could do nothing and therefore soon after made his retreat. The marks of the Guru's body are still etched on this boulder, and we often go there to worship, every year in the last week of the month of March, because that is the month when the Guru is said to have come here. A fair is held to commemmerate Guru Nanak's visit. Quite close to the boulder, there is a cave, through which the Guru used to pass to have his bath in the rivulet called Bamchu. Again, it is commonly believed by us all that it is only the people with a clean heart who can pass through the cave. Others, no matter how lean they are, cannot pass through the entrance of the cave.

The Lama continued with his story; "The place where the Guru used to have his bath in the rivulet is now a natural shallow pool which is full of small black as well as white pebbles, and the water is always still. Whenever we want to know whether or not any particular wish of ours is going to be fullfilled, we close our eyes, repeat the wish, pray to Guru Nanak, and pick out a pebble from the pool. If the pebble is white, we believe, this wish is bound to come true. If the pebble is black, it will not be. If it has both black and white spots on it, the wish will be only partially fulfilled. You can try any number of times, the colour of the pebble you pick out once is always the same later'.

I must say I was quite intrigued by the lama's story and persuaded him to take me there. He agreed and next morning we set out. In order to get to Pemoshubu, we had to pass through a thick forest which was known to be infested with bears, tigers and wild boars. The track had vanished under the undergrowth and we had to cut the waggling branches to clear our way to the place in the dense jungle. In the midst of the thick undergrowth, we found a small clearing where the traditional white Bodhi flag, printed with 'On Mani Padam Hum' was aflutter. The lama told me of Bodhi belief that every time the flag flutters, God's name goes into the air 1001 times.

From the clearing, we started our descent towards the Bumchu river. After walking down for about five minutes, we came across a huge boulder which appeared to be about 30 feet high and with a length and breadth each of about 20 feet. It was leaning towards the east. Below it, there was a sort of rough platform on which were lying a number of white cloth flags with inscriptions on them in the Tibetan language.

The lama bowed in deep reverence and then started to ring his bell and chant hymns. He also laid on the platform a new white cloth flag as his offering. He then showed the marks of the body etched on the boulder; they were about ten feet above the ground. There appeared the impressions of two bodies etched on the boulder - one of a bigger man and the other of a smaller one. The Lama told me that the bigger one was that of Guru Nanak's and the smaller one of his companion. The impress of the head, the shoulders, the arms and the upper part of the body was very clear. It did not look as if they had been chiselled but naturally hewn. Since I had no means of verifying the veracity of these marks, I accepted what the Lama said, and bowed my head in reverence.

After that, the lama took me further down through a cave, and from its farther end we could see the beautiful rivulet, Bamchu flowing by down below. At one corner lay the pool ; its water was quite transparent, I could clearly see the white and black pebbles lying at the bottom.

The Lama bent over the small pool. Muttering Guru Nanak's name, he took out a stone out of the pool, he got a white one. He was too happy. when I enquired as to what he had wished, he told that he had wished for another son. I was astonished at his material attachment despite of being a Lama. A Junior Commissioned officer Subedar Surat Singh Yadav who accompanied us, too dipped his arm into the pool but got a black stone. He was sad. He had prayed for becoming a Subedar Major, and I knew it was not possible for him to become one. They both insisted that I too try for one. I had nothing on mind as God has always been kind to me. However, a momentous thought came to me, 'why not wish to make a place of worship at the place?' Having wished, I took out a pebble and found it to be white. When I pondered over the complete question, I considered it impossible to construct a place of worship alone at such a remote place, where leave alone bringing up the material from the low lands in Assam, reaching and cleaning the forests were the major problems. I thought it better to consider it as a bad joke.

However my Subedar was quick to respond. "There will have to be a place for the Guru here", he assuringly said. "But how can I alone make a place in such a difficult area?", I raised my doubt. "Why you alone Sahib? We all will make it", added the burly Subedar. "We will make

Guru Nanak's place here. It is His wish", said the Lama authoritatively. I was in a divided state of mind, but the other two had already started playing this idea on their minds seriously.

"We should not alter the originality and serenity of this place and keep it as it is", said Subedar Surat Singh. "Better place will be the triangular area between the two rivulets. That is within the limits as prescribed by the religious edicts". Subedar Surat Singh further said. "It should be within 500 yards of the place of event", he explained. I was unaware of all this. As we walked across to the place and examined the area, I found the Lama to be in meditation sitting on a stone. I found the area to be flat but full of big trees and with thick under growth. However, it was not slushy because of the close flowing stream and the slope of the land into these streams.

It required lot of effort to clear it. For bringing stores, this place was another very difficult preposition as even nails would have to be got from Tinsukhia, which for ordinary person would have taken 10-15 days journey one way. The other alternative was through air, i.e., helicopters, but their priority was the ration for jawans and ammunition for guns than anything else. In addition, the carriage of these items for 16 kilometers from the heliped was another difficulty. The first requirement, however was to clear the thick under growth upto the selected place which itself was a major task. I did not think it feasible to prepare a worthwhile place of worship, under these conditions.

"This is an auspicious place. 15 days hence is the auspicious day to lay the stone for the place of worship, the Lama announced keeping his eyes closed. "Perfectly alright. We will clear the place within that time", Subedar Surat Singh took upon himself voluntarily, the preliminery task of clearing the area and also the track to the place. The area was studied minutely and the place was selected where the Lama finally put a small stick and a small piece of cloth bearing 'Om Mani Padme Hum' hanging over it as a flag. As we returned, Subedar Surat Singh studied the route seriously. The Lama told us whom all to contact locally for construction of the place of worship. I thought of it as to how I could get the building meterial. It was better to make a wooden structure which should consist of at least three rooms, one for the main worship, one for the sevadar/religious man and one for store and other accessories. This could also be used for any person from outside who wished to stay. It would require about 800 wooden planks and about 100 C.G.I. sheets in addition to other building material. "How can we manage this all"? I passed on the question to Subedar Surat Singh. Nothing seemed to unruffle the Subedar as he seemed to be quite determined. "We will prepare the planks ourselves by sawing wood. C.G.I. sheets can be arranged by air", he said as if it was not difficult at all. On return, Subedar Surat Singh was heard stating the whole incident to the men of my unit with lot of enthusiasm. These deeply religious Ahirs of Harayana, took every word stated by Subedar Surat Singh seriously and gave a word to him that they will do every bit to carry out the "Will of God".

The work started without delay and the men, who were eager to do something worthwhile, swung into action. Meanwhile the Lama had told Segang people about the event. The Gaon Burha came with his men to help us in whatever way we wanted to utilise him. Subedar Surat Singh asked for the help of a carpenter and a sawman which the Gaon Burha deputed without hitch. I requested him to get the land transferred to the institution which he agreed heartily. He alongwith the Lama planned to meet the Extra Assistant Commissioner, Manchuka for permission and transfer of the land on the name of the institution.

Work started the very same day with clearing part of the route by the Jawans and a group of villagers. I wrote a letter to my wife in Dinjan Assam giving all the details and requesting her to buy the required number of C.G.I. sheets and other materials and to arrange the money for the same. Bringing the material to Manchukha from Dinjan-Tinsukhia was certainly a problem. I thought of it for 2 - 3 days when I met the pilot of the helicopter providing us supplies. He too was eager to visit the place. I took him through the difficult route. After paying his obeissance he saw the area around closely and mentioned that about 500 yards away, there was a good ground, which sould be developed into a dropping zone and if some effort is put in, it can also be converted into a helipad. For this, permission and clearance had to come from higher headquarters.

The work progressed faster than expected. Soonafter the Assam Rifles jawans also joined our jawans and both the track and the area were cleared within a week. The seniormost offieer of the area was the

Batallion Commander of Mahar Regiment and at that time Major Yadav, again an Ahir, was officiating. As I told him about the place, he too went there out of curiosity. Visiting the area, he recommended deploying a company on the nearby hill as he found it to be yet an unknown route from the enemy side and needed an immediate coverage. The development of the area turned out to be much faster than I would have ever expected. Later the higher commanders of Army, Air Force and Assam Rifles, who visited Manchuka, made it a point to visit the place. With the help of the local carpenters and jawans, three rooms were constructed. A company of Engineers landed which not only improved the local constructions but was also given the task of preparing an Advance Landing Ground for the aeroplanes as well as helipads and tracks/roads to various locations. Soon the guns were moved just close to the place of worship. The place was given the name 'Guru Nanak Taposthan' and had become a great place of worship not only for the local people but for all the outsiders as well, who longed to carry some worthwhile memories back home.

There was a big fair of the local people at the place on 24 March (1977), as this was the occasion on which Guru Nanak had come to the place. We arranged to give free lunch for all the people visiting the place and had shabad-kirtan organised. Sri Guru Granth Sahib too had been placed by then which I got on one of my visits to Tinsukhia. Initially, I carried out the daily routine prayers and rituals at the place in which the Lama helped me. Later a jawan from the Engineer company took over the task on himself.

We celebrated Baisakhi with all rituals as the jawans of the Engineers company comprised of Sikhs who took keen interest in performing the rituals. We were able to have an Akhand Path' i.e., 'non-stop recitation of the entire "Sri Guru Granth Sahib" within 48 hours'.

From Pemoshubu, Guru Nanak visited various places in Menchukha Valley here is a hill at Segong-Dorgilling on the top of which there is one Gonpha (Lama Temple), Alongwith Lord Buddha's Idol has a life-sized idol of Guru Nanak, which the Membas (local people) worship. A regular fair is held in the month of January at this place. A Lama told the author, "The monastry had a book of Guru's shabads in their language which was destroyed in a fire about fifty years ago". The Head Lama of this monastry had been visiting Gaya as well as Amritsar.

Guru Nanak is said to have visited Shekhar-Bhumju and Dargilling as well. Regular fairs are held in February at these places. Fairs coincide with the dates of Guru Nanak's visit to these places. Calculation of the days and dates is as per Tibetan calender.

Close to Menchukha, there is a snow-white cave. Guru Nanak is said to have meditated in this cave also. It is said that Guru Nanak stayed in this area for about 3 months.

According to the local Membas, Guru Nanak brought them from Southern Tibet and got them settled in the valley where they are far better off from their previous place. In their songs they give out the legend, how they were brought to Menchukha by Guru Nanak.

From Menchukha, Guru Nanak proceeded towards Gelling and Tuting via South-Eastern Tibet along Tsangpo river. Guru Nanak is worshipped in the Gompha of Gelling-Tuting valley too.

From Gelling-Tuting valley, Guru Nanak proceeded along Tsangpo (Siang River) and then crossed over to Sadiya. Near Sadiya, there is a place known as Bhishmaknagar, where Lord Krishna was married to Rukhmini. Wife of Lord Krishna was the daughter of King Bhihmak, whose marriage was planned to another king while she wanted to marry Lord Krishna only. Lord Krishna abducted her and married her at Malinithan, a place near Likabali in the presence of Lord Shiva and Parvati. Old temples are reminiscent of the event. From Sadia Guru Nanak went to Tezu and reached Brahmkund on Kartika Purnima. Here he attended the fair, held in honour of Parasuram, who is said to have carved out Brahamputra from the Brahamkund.

From Brahama kund, Guru Nanak visited Walong at the eastern edge of Arunachal Pradesh. He is said to have visited Rima in China from here. Therefrom, he returned to Tinsukhia and Dibrugarh to Sibsagar. At Tinsukhia, the followers of Sankara Deb regularly visit Gurudwara on Guru Nanak's Birthday in honour of Guru's visit to the area and call Guru Nanak as Guru Bhai of Shankardev. About 18 KM from Sibsagar, there are ruins of an old kingdom (Swaranpur), which Guru Nanak is said to have visited and held discussions with the ruler of the place who became Guruji's disciple.

On further enquiries during visits and from the study of the books I could link up Guru Nanak's visit to Arunachal with that of Sikkim and Bhutan. On the basis of information collected, I visited Bhutan and Eastern Arunachal in 1988 and 89 and collected more information from Sela, Tawang, Lumla, Zimithang Lumpung and other parts of this country.

According to this information, from Hajo (in Assam) Guru Nanak went to Bhutan and visited Tashigong-Dzong and Dukti. Therefrom he entered Arunachal Pradesh via Lumla. 'He visited Sela and Sabrela and crossed a hill now known as Govindgarh. From there, he visited a place now known as Nanak Dzong. He stayed at the place for some days and held discourses. There the people worship him till today as Nanak Lama[1].

Thereafter he proceeded further North and visited the famous monastry at Tawang. His painting is still preserved at the monastry. The Lamas worship Guru Nanak as their Guru Rimpoche[2]; 'As he went further on the route adopted by Dalai lama while escaping from Lhasa, he relaxed on a boulder and enjoyed the beauty of the nature. This boulder is marked by its speciality that even during heavy snow fall, it remains uncovered while the snow engulfs every inch of the area upto six feet in winter'[3]. He crossed over Jhagla ridge later lenown as 'Nankeyen-Jhagla' and recorded so in maps. 'Guru Nanak then went to Nagula, where he meditated for some time. Now, a meditation centre has been established for all religions in memory of Guru Nanak's visit to the place[2]'. When I visited Lumpung monastry and met the head Lama there, he told me that Guru Nanak reached Lumpung en route to Lhasa from Twang and stayed at the place for sometime. He showed me a large sized statue of about 20 feet and stated it to be of Guru Nanak which I photographed. He also told me the route adopted by Guru Nanak to the place and to Lhasa which was more or less the same as adopted by Dalai Lama during his departure from Lhasa.

Lhasa (Tibet)

Guru Nanak again entered Tibet from Nagula and reached Lhasa. At Lhasa, Guru Nanak visited the famous Potala, the seat of Dalai Lama.

At that time, the power was transferred from Kar-ma-pa sect to Ge-lug-pa sect. The Ge-lug-pa sect had started a reign of terror against the Kar-ma-pa sect, the sect which had become the follower of Guru Nanak.

Guru Nanak is stated to have held discussion with the Second Dalai Lama at Potala and requested him to stop blood-shed. During the stay at Lhasa, he visited the famous monastries there. In one of the monastries, where Guru Nanak was offered refreshement, made comfortable and approached with a request for answer to certain questions. He answered these questions with great magnanimity.

> "How can we reach the Absolute?", asked the Lama. The Guru replied; "As a beggar goes abegging, bowl in one hand and staff in the other, rings in his ears, in ashes smothered, so you go forth in life with ear-rings made of contentment, with modesty your begging bowl, meditation the fabric of your garment, knowledge of death your cowl, let your mind be chaste, virginal humility, with mind subdue, the world subjugate (Japji P-6). The Lama was very much satisfied and pleased.

At Lhasa, Guru Nanak was told about another famous monastry in South East. The monastry was known as Samya Monastry. The famous religious centre and the centre of teaching of Kar-ma-pa sect. Guru Nanak proceeded towards Samya monastry and enroute halted near Cherisarma. There a capshaped peak is worshipped by the local people. They go around this hill as if doing Parikarma of Sri Harimandar Sahib. The capshaped peak is believed to be the Seli Topi (cap) of Guru Nanak which the Guru left to protect the hill and people there, from demons.

At Samya monastry Guru Nanak held discussions with the Lamas. From Samya, Guru Nanak came to La Khanya and entered India (Arunachal Pradesh) along Yargapchu river into Pemoshubu. Menchuka Valley a thick natural forest area, where beautiful flowers are found in bountiful.

From Menchukha to Assam his route throughKongbo-Dakbo, Tutinggelling-Saiduja-Bhishmekunagar Walong, Brahma-kund and Tinsukhia has been as described earlier.

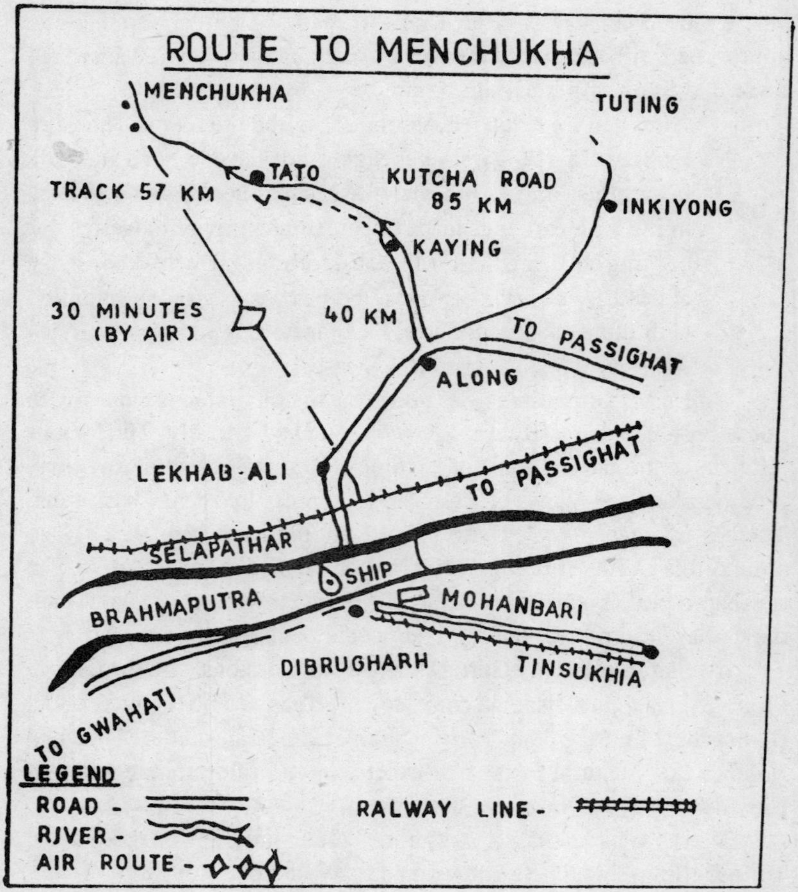
ROUTE TO MENCHUKHA
MENCHUKHA
TUTING
TATO
KUTCHA ROAD
85 KM
TRACK 57 KM
INKIYONG
KAYING
30 MINUTES
(BY AIR)
40 KM
TO PASSIGHAT
ALONG
LEKHAB-ALI
TO PASSIGHAT
SELAPATHAR
SHIP
BRAHMAPUTRA
MOHANBARI
DIBRUGHARH
TINSUKHIA
TO GWAHATI
LEGEND
ROAD -
RJVER -
AIR ROUTE -
RALWAY LINE -

GURU NANAK AT MENCHUKHA (ALONG) ARUNACHAL PRADESH

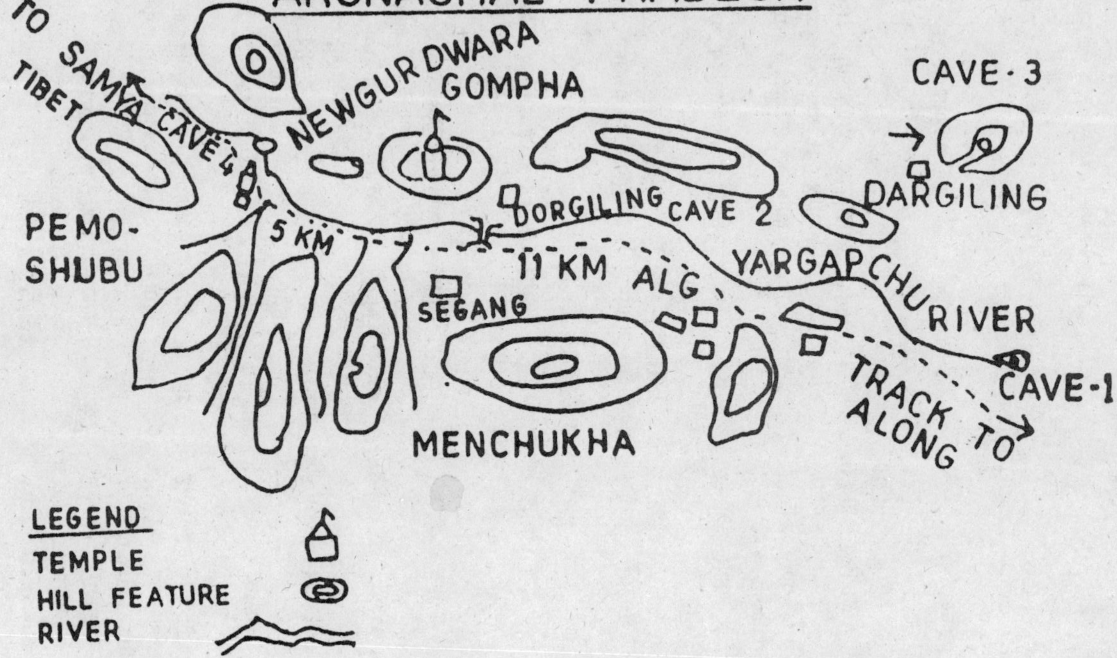

Places in Arunachal Pradesh Connected with Guru Nanak Distance & Time Chart

	From	To	Distance (oneway)	Terrain	Mode	Time	Accommo dation
1.	Delhi	Gwahati	2000km	Plain	Air& Train	3 hrs 26 hrs	Hotels Gurdwara
2.	Gwahati	Bomblila		Hilly	Bus	10 hrs	Hotels
3.	Bomdila	Tawang	171km	Hilly	Bus Taxi	2 days	Hotels
4.	Tawang	Zimithang Lumpung	-	High Altitude	Manpack	3 days	own
5.	Gwahati	North Lakhimpur	-	Plain	Train Bus	5 hrs	Hotels
6.	North aekhimpur	Along	-	Hilly	Bus	6 hrs	Hotels
7.	Along	Kayeeng	40 kms	Hilly	Bus	1hr	self contained
8.	Kayeeng	Menchukha	85km	Hilly	Manpack	7 days	self contained
9.	Gwahati	Dibrugarh	562kms	Plain Bus Train	Air From Mohan-Bari		Hotels
10.	Dibrugarh	Menchukha	175km	Hilly	Air	30 mts	Self-Contained
11.	Dibrugarh	Tuting	215kms	Hilly	Air	30 mts	-do-
	Mohanbari	Walong	180 Kms	Hilly	Air	30 mts	-do-
12.	Gwahati	Tinsukhia	515 Kms	Plain	Train Bus	17 hrs 10 hrs	Hotels
13.	Tinsukhia	Tezu (Brahamkund)	-	Hilly	Bus	3 hrs	Self-Contained

References

1. Surinder Singh (Dr.), *'Travels of Guru Nanak'*, P.
2. Ibid
3. Ibid

Assam

The land of Mighty Brahamputra banked by lush green tree gardens and tropical forests, Assam is the North-Eastern State of India bounded by Tibet and Bhutan in the north, Burma and China in the east, Burma in the south and Eengal and Bangla Desh in the west. Earlier a composite State with a total area of 9 millions miles, is now divided into 7 states territories i.e. the states of Assam, Manipur, Maghalayas, Nagaland, Tripura, Arunachal Pradesh and Mizoram.

For the present study, all these states shall be considered as one except Arunachal Pradesh which has been dealt separately.

Assam earlier known as Kamrup was considered less developed and less civilised. Magic and idol worship prevailed and the Gods and spirits were dreaded and worshipped to the scale that even human sacrifice was resorted to appease them. Hieun Tsang, the famous Chinese Traveller who visited Assam in 640 A.D., wrote about this country 'The country of Kamarupa is about 10,000 Li (nearly 1800 miles) in circuit. The capital town is 5 miles round. The land lies low but is rich and regularly cultivated. The climate is soft and temperate. The men are of small stature and their complexion dark yellow. Their language differs a little from that of mid-India. Their nature is very impetuous and wild, their memories are retentive and they are earnest in study. The name of the present king who is Brahmin by caste, is Kumar Bhaskar Varma'.

Today Karmrup is the name of a district only and the old Kamrup Kingdom has come to be known as Assam. Before Bhaskar Varman, the dynasty of Narkasur and Bhagyadatt remained supreme for long. According to Mahabhart, king of Pragjyotishar (Gwahati) led his army to the battle of Kuruksheter.

For several centuries the Koch, the Ahoms and the Chutians contested for Assam, but in the early part of the 13th century the Ahoms from Burma and the Chinese frontiers poured into Assam, founded a kingdom and held it for several centuries. The Ahoms were in the process of establishment and routing out the local Hindu Kings during the period of Guru Nanak's visit to Assam. The ferocious Ahoms, had unleashed a reign of terror and practised all savagery on the local population to subdue them. Guru's entry into Assam at that period was quite solacing. He visited all these states and encouraged the people to stand against the tyranny and to shed away the meaningless ritualism and caste distinctions.

Guru Nanak entered Assam twice once while coming down from Bhutan and entered Lhasa snd second time while coming down from Eastern Arunachal Pradesh.

After having travelled Central Bhutan, Guruji descended to East Bengal and through Cooch Behar, he reached Dhubri.

He practically visited all the towns of lower and upper Assam and reached Saidya, Brahamkund, Tibet, China, Japan, Java Sumatra, Phillipines and Manipore states through Burma. He entered India at Imphal, Baghnapora, Cachar, Syllhet and Lushai Hills.[1]

At Dhubri, there used to be a huge hillock on the bank of Brahamputra river, the Guru is said to have meditated here and held discussions with Shri Sankar-deb. Gurdwara Damdama Sahib is reminiscent of Guru's visit to this place. Sri Sarkardeb's (1449-1569) name is a household word in Assam. He was born at Bardoa village of Nowgong and was brought up according to Hindu traditions. He came in contact with sages on a pilgrimage and his mental make-up got transformed for the search of the Ultimate Truth. His life history and basic principles of thought process are very akin to Guru Nanak Dev's.

He lived the life of a householder and stood for truth. He opposed all meaningless rituals and ceremonies of the time. He preached a simple faith. The cardinal power in his faith is chanting of the name of God. According to him, the worship of many gods and goddesses is unnecessary, the same Supreme Soul exists in all beings. There can be no two classes of touchables and untouchables. Devotion and not salvation is the aim of human life.

These principles known to Assamese as Eksarana Dharma seemed to have been embedded in him during the discussions with Guru Nanak at Dhubri. The followers of Sri Sankra-Deb known as Mahapursh sect till date consider Guru Nanak as 'Guru Bhai' of Sri Sankar Deb and attend religious functions in various Gurdwaras held in honour of Guru Nanak.

Dhubri was later visited by Guru Tegh Bahadur where he brought a settlement between Raja Ram Singh General of Mughals and King Chakardhawaj Singh of Assam.

From Dhubri Guru Nanak proceeded towards Guwahati through Gauripore, Ramgamati, Jogigompha, and Goalpara.

At Kamakhaya the famous temple of Guwahati, he stayed with 'Panjabi Panda' and held discussions with various pandits including the head priest. Old wahis of Punjabi Panda had a mention about Guru's visit but were destroyed in a fire at his house. Now records are available with him only from Ninteenth century onwards. There are two different views about the legend of Mardana's conversion to a lamb. While some writers attribute this to a place named Dhanpur (near Dacca) now in Bangladesh, Dr. Tarlochan Singh[2] relates this incidence to Gwahati. According to him Mardana was made a lamb by Noor Shah at Gwahati. Mardana eager to see the town, proceeded alone, by taking permission from Guru Nanak. At that time Guwahati was said to be ruled by a queen. An indication to this is available in 'The Background of Assamese Culture' by S.K. Bhuyan as follows.

"A state is stated to have existed in a certain part of the country inhabited only by women, governed by a woman ruler with the help of women ministers and soldiers, and any male stranger unknowingly stepping into it was sapped to death"[3]. Sujan Rai mentions the prevalence of magic in Kamrup stating as follows,' 'The women of this place are extremely beautiful. They are expert in magic. They make roofs and pillars of the houses with the human bodies. These men can breathe but cannot move with their magic. These women turn men to sheep, tigers or animals or birds. Tail and ear appear on human bodies like animals. These women can win anyone's heart with magic'.[4]

As Mardana entered the town, the local women converted Mardana into a lamb and tied him up under a roof. After the long wait for return of Mardana, Guru Nanak himself left for the city to search for him. The magic women among whom Noor Shah was the chief, were pleased to find Guru Nanak in their net.

They tried all tricks of magic on the Guru but failed. They realised that the Guru was a great saint and no ordinary person. Meanwhile Guru Nanak proceeded to Mardana and broke the thread from his neck. The magic spell broke and Mardana turned into his original shape of a man.

Noor Shah and the other women, soon recognised their folly and fell at Guru's feet and requested His forgiveness which he gave without reservation. He established a place for religious meetings and prayers (Dharamsal) at Gwahati and proceeded towards Hajo, another religious centre. He visited Matsayadhavaj, where a temple exists in honour of Lord Vishnu. Mardana Kund and Bala Kund commemmorate Guru's visit to this place[5].

From Hajo and Matsayadhwaj Guru Nanak proceeded to Tashigongzong (Bhutan) on his way to Lhasa (Tibet) and Samye Monastry (Tibet). From there he proceeded to Saidya and attended the fair at Brahma Kund. After religious discussions at Brahmankund, the Guru proceeded to Walong and held discussions the with the Lama there. Therefrom he returned to Assam and visited Tinsukhia, Dibrugarh and Sibsagar.

At Sibsagar he met the local ruler and held discussions with him in the foot. The ruler became which is now in ruins Guru's disciple. Guru Nanak visited neighbouring villages and preached True Lord's Name to them.

From Sibasagar, Guru Nanak came towards Jorhat and Dhansiri River area and reached Golaghat on the bank of river Dhansiri. A Gurdwara at Golaghat commemorates Guru's visit to the place. From Golaghat, Guru Nanak entered Nagaland. In this area, 'there is a tribe which call themselves as Nanak tribe'. They are very free minded and paid no taxes to their than king.[6]

Human sacrifice was rempant in Lohit District and Nagaland at that time. As late as 1958, this writer has come across a case of human sacrifice in Arunchal Pradesh. Near Sadya, there used to be a Kali Temple, where human beings were sacrified till 1948. This was later banned by Government orders.

Their method of human sacrifices as told to the author by the local people of Lohit district was very gruesome. During the inter-tribal feuds, the individuals were made captive and the ojhas' (local Priests) used to select a person suitable for sacrifice. The selected person was given a special kind of reed to eat which made the person fat and soft, so soft that he was unable to run and easy to cut. During the day of the ritual, proper prayers were performed by 'the Ojha in the Kali Temple and the man was sacrificed with a single blow of dah (a cutting weapon) amidst the beating of the drums. The meat and blood were offered to the Goddess and also distributed as prasad (offering).

Record of this system is available in the Imperial Gazetteer as well. 'The custom which has attracted most attention and which differentiates Nagas from other Tibet Burman tribes such as Bodos, Mikirs and Daflas and such was their craving for the human heads that any head was valued, whether of man, woman or child and victims were usually murdered not in fight but by treachery'. (Imperial Gazetteer of India, volume 18, P-287).

The legends connected with Kauda Rakshash is also stated to have occured in Nagaland[6].

Janamsakhi Walait Walli (P.44), Janamsakhi Meharban (P.121), Janamsakhi Bhai Balla (P.259-260) and Janamsakhi Bhai Mani Singh (P-352-3), all have a record of the event, while passing through the wild area, Mardana felt hungry and asked for the permission of Guru Nanak to search for food. The Guru warned him "There are wild men living in this forest, so be careful where you go'

"You are Nanak Nirankari, God's own," said Mardana. "You are not affected with hunger and pain. I am a mere man and subjected to both".

Mardana had gone a few furlongs, when Kauda, a notorious Rakhshas, met him. Kauda kept oil boiling in a big pan to roast his victims. He saw Mardana from a distance. He was delighted at a prospect of a good flesh. He took Mardana by surprise and in an instance tied him with rope. Kauda then carried him to a spot where his pot was boiling.

Mardana now prayed to the Guru to save him. The Guru already knew of his distress and was on his way to help him. He arrived just at the time when Kauda was preparing to throw him into the boiling pot.

Kauda stopped as he saw two men approaching him. He thought he had two more victims. He rushed towards them swinging his rope.

As he approached, the Guru raised his hand and Kauda stopped, trembling from head to foot and then fell on the ground unable to move, looking helplessly with his large wild eyes at the Guru and entirely bewildered. Bala released Mardana.

Then the Guru turned to Kauda and commanded him to rise. Kauda slowly raised himself and then fell at eh feet of the Guru and prayed for mercy. He said, "It has been foretold that a man, "of God will save my soul".

"God is all-merciful," said the Guru, "He is all compassion. He forgives all those who repent and refrain from doing wrong".

"I will do as you bid me, "said Kauda, "accept me as your disciple".

"Listen," said the Guru, "and act on what I tell you and thus win grace, Learn; attachment, greed, anger and harmfulness are the four streams of fire. These consume mankind. Only virtuous action can quench the fire and open treasures of bliss".

"From now onward resolve to harm no one, be merciful and serve all those who need your service. Concentrate your mind on the creator, learn to love him with all your heart and mind, just as lovers do, and make His name, the sustenance of your life".

Kauda was converted completely and till the end of his days acted as a devout disciple of the Guru.[7]

"From Nagaland, Guru Nanak visited Imphal, Silchar, Brahampur, Sonpur, Bishanpur, Ajmeri Ganj, Karimganj and Ghoragaon enroute to Sylhet'.[8]

'While at Chchar, Guru Nanak paid a visit to a Budhist Sangharam Monastry at Bhuvan Hill about 32 Km from the town of Silchar, (the Sadar of Cachar District). The Chief controller of that Temple, when heard about the effectiveness of the Guru's sermons, was full of jealousy. With a drawn sword in hand in order to kill Guru Nanak he rushed to the place where Guru Nanak was sitting. Guru uttered a Hymn in the vernacular of the head Priest.

'Whomsoever God gives protection, no body can kill him. Nanak says, one who envies a saint of God, he goes to hell.'

'On hearing this, the Head Priest could not strike the blow, and his mind was instantly changed from the evil design. He humbly asked for forgiveness which was granted by Guru Nanak. He was so influenced that he became follower of the Guru. There was a small place called Nanak Ghar, near the place but there was no temple. Only an enclosure of trees existed. There was one Mahatma looking after the place[9].

From Silchar Guru Nanak proceeded to syllhet (Bengaladesh) via Brahampur, Sonpur, Bishanpur, Ajmeriganj, Karimganj and Ghoragaon.

References

1. Dr. Arjun Singh Mann, *'Guru Tegh Bahadur and Assam Pradesh'* Sikh Publishing House, New Delhi, Ist edn 1959, P-179.
2. Trilochan Singh (Dr), *Jiwan Charitar Guru Nanak Devji,* P.168
3. Bhuyan S.K. The background of Assamese Culture.
4. Sujan Rai, *'Khulasul Twarikh'*
5. Dr. Arjun Singh Mann, *'Guru Tegh Bahadur and Assam Pradesh'* P.179.
6. Mohammad Kazim 'A discription of Assam', Asiatic Researches, Vol I, P-118.
7. Trilochan Singh (Dr) *Jeeven Charitar Guru Nanak Devji,* P-172-3.
8. Surinder Singh Kohli (Dr), *'Travels of Guru Nanak'.* P-49.
9. Arjan Singh Mann, P-179.

East Asian Countries Including China

Guru Nanak's journey to East Asia and China has not been explored despite the evidence available to the fact that Guru Nanak visited China and the place 'Nanking' is named after Guru Nanak's Name[1]. In various Janamsakhis also, the accounts are available describing Guru Nanak's journey to 'Brahampur', 'Silmila Dweep'[2] and numerous other Dweeps (Islands). His journey by sea is well explained by Dr. Kohli,[3] which leaves no doubt that Guru Nanak visited East of Assam by land and sea. The countries visited by him in East Asia are a subject of study here.

East Asia includes countries of Burma, Thailand, Malaysia, Indonesia, Kampuchea, Vietnam, Philippines, Japan, Korea and China. Both Budhism as well as Muslim religion are prevalent in these countries. During his journey towards the East, Guru Nanak is stated to have visited Burma, Thailand, Malaya; Peninsula, Jawa, Sumatra and even parts of China. The area covered by Malaya Peninsula, Jawa Sumatra etc; was known as Salmala Dwipa.[4] At the time of Guru Nanak's journey, exploration work of Islands was already in progress. Indians have gone far into these countries and evidence is available of trade and transit of Indians via sea. India had a pride of place among these countries. It was known as the originator of Buddhism, the reverred place of Lord Buddha. India was also the most developed and culturally and economically rich nation. These countries looked forward to India for spiritual guidance as well. Guru Nanak proceeded to these countries from Assam in the years 1616-1617 and travelled both by land and by sea. The details are available in the Janamsakhis. Describing the area, Janamsakhi mentions "When Mardana, the companion of the Guru, expressed his desire to see all the seven dweeps the Guru said, "The great Jambu dweep is spread over one lakh yojan and lies in the middle of other dweeps. The great mountain Sumeru lies within it. You have already seen the nine regions of this

Dweep and one of these regions is Bharata Varsha. I cannot refuse to show you the other dweeps, therefore, let us go". Then the Guru started on this great journey.

An ocean, one lakh yojan in length was crossed within a short period, the Guru reached Plaksha Dweep with his companions. This dweep was named after white Plaksha (or Pakhar) tree which was found in abundance in this region. The word Plaksha in Sanskrit means white. The people in this region were white and lustrous and lived a comfortable life like gods. They lived upto one thousand years. This dweep was divided into seven parts and had seven rivers.

Several people of the dweep gathered round the Guru considering him a holy man from another dweep and presented fruits of the area. The Guru asked them about the general condition of life in their dweep. They said, "We have all comforts of life, but we have certain vices which create troubles. Jealousy is created on seeing the superiors, ego is created on seeing inferiors and enemity on seeing the equals. If these vices are shed away, there will be bliss for ever. Kindly suggest some remedy for these ills."

The Guru said, "There is light of God within everybody and there is none without Him. If you think in this way, the inequality will cease. There will be no trouble. Remember the name of the Lord. Join the holy congregation as brothers and pray". The people of the dweep became his followers.

After staying there for several days, the Guru proceeded to the next dweep after crossing the Plaksha dweep spread over two lakh yojans. Then there was an ocean of sugarcane-juice, two lakh yojans in length which was crossed by the Guru and his companions. They remained thirsty throughout this journey. They then entered the next dweep ie, Salmali Dweep. This dweep derived its name from Salmali (Simmal) or silk-cotton tree. The Guru visited the town in this dweep. The people and the king received him with great respect. The Guru initiated the king and his subject into his discipline.[5] Details as given in Janamsakhi Bhai Balla are as follows:-

'There is a foreign country named Asrapan under a king. Guru Nanak started his journey to the place. There is a seat of Jhanda Badhi over there. They moved to Bisihar Desh which is on an island in the ocean... They moved ahead... It was a journey for fifteen days and nights. All three survived on air. Thereafter they reached Bisihar Desh, where Sudharsain was the king."[6] Guru Nanak blessed Jhanda Badhi and Indersain in Bisihar Desh. Jhanda Badhi a carpenter by trade, was appointed as preacher in the area. Indersain who was the nephew of king Sudharsain was enlightened by Guru's teaching and became his life long disciple. Janamsakhi further records :-

"Then king Sudharsain got the news of Guru Nanak's arrival. He said to his courtiers, "A saint has come to my city who has been accepted as Guru by Jhanda Badhi. Please bring him to me.... He proceeded to Guru Nanak and bowing before him gave whatever he had brought. Inderersain spoke, "Sire, the king is great indeed. You must bless him." Guru Nanak then blessed him and sang a shabad in Raag Bilawal, *'Mite aandh aag gaye bikara. Aisa sahib meet hamara'*. (All blindness, fire of desire and vices vanish after meeting the great Lord, whom we love.)

King Sudharsain then ruled hundred islands for hundred years. There were eighteen other kings over which he ruled. He ruled three dweeps on the name of Guru Nanak and became a great person... Guru Nanak stayed with king Sudharsain and Jhanda Badhi for one month on the request of Indersain.

Therefrom they (Guru Nanak, Bala and Mardana) proceeded to Silmilla dweep. They moved on vast stretch of waters of the sea as if they were moving on earth. It took six months for them to reach. While they reached Silmilla Dweep, Guru Nanak's name was already well known. Everyone narrated how he bestowed upon Sudharsain the kingdom of three dweeps and how he made Jhanda Badhi a great saint.

All three stayed in the garden of a city. Mardana desired to go to the city. In fact he was eager to have some food from the city. Guru Nanak said, "The name of this city is Brahampur and is ruled by Madhurbain." As they were discussing, Raja Madhurbain turned up there hunting. He questioned them. When he found that they were accompanied by the saint who has been to Bisihar to bless Sudharsain with a kingdom, he was very much pleased. He gave out details of his kingdom and surounding areas. He stated, "I am Madhurbain, I am the king of this area and a Brahaman by caste. Name of this city is Brahampur. ...There are eighteen kings in these three dweeps. They are Kaulnain, Madhurbain, Sudhersain,

Sukhchain, Asrapan, Sagarsain, Birnain, Lalnain, Raisain, Sukhsagar, Naga Paras Ram, Raja Atka-Ghatka, Sudhibalka, Budh-Bibek-Balka, Raja Nam Jyoti, Raja Bali Sanghar, Raja Jur Jarang and Raja Madan Raja". Bala told him, "Guru Nanak has blessed Sudharsain to rule over all of you. Raja Madhurbain invited Guru Nanak to city. Guru Nanak sang sabad in raag Bilaval *'Ek Bhandar nam ke jin sabh kichh dia, bhukh nang sabh cheenkar apna kar liya'* (God his given me every thing by giving me the store of True Name. He has snatched hunger and nakedness and made me his own). Raja Madhurbain then became his disciple. Guru Nanak asked him to serve Sudharsain. All three stayed with Madhurbain for one month before departing.

While travelling through sea for thirty seven days and ninghts, they saw a city, named Deogandhar. Its ruler was Devloot, who ruled 17 lakh gods. He was a cannibal. As he heard the news of all three sitting outside his city, he ordered his soldiers to bring them for his food. When the soldiers came to arrest them, they were unable to see Guru and his companions. On the failure of soldiers, Devloot himself tried but he too was unable to see Guru. One of his minister, Devdoot, told Devloot, "The saint seems to be a person of great divine power. Let me go with no ill feeling and see what happens. If I too get blinded, you can do to me whatever you wish." The king Devloot agreed. As Devdoot went with pure heart he could see Guru Nanak and his companions. He asked Guru Nanak, "Who are you? From where and for what purpose have you come here?" Guru Nanak stated Amar Nagar as his residence and Nanak Nirankari as his name. The minister requested him to go to the city alongwith. This Guru Nanak refused stating that he being a saint was happy wherever, he was. ...The minister told the complete details to the King Devloot. But the king, adamant to hunt upon the Guru, said, "Let us all go. In case I am able to catch him, you will be punished." As they all went, all except the minister became blind again. Raja Devloot was repentent of his act. He prayed to Guru Nanak to excuse him. At this Guru Nanak asked him to open his eyes. Astonishingly on opening his eyes the King found Guru Nanak in front of him. Guru Nanak then asked him to change his food habits, to stop cannibalism and to consider all men equal. He also asked him to follow King Sudharsain. He stayed there for nine months.

His next visit was to Prasar Nama city. It was a three months journey. This area was ruled by King Teekhantain the king of apes. These apes used to live on wild-animal-hunt and jungle food. Seeing Guru Nanak and his companions, all except one ran. The one who stopped, presented a tasty fruit which they enjoyed.

Next journey was for seven months and thirteen days to another island. Guru Nanak and Bala sat outside the premises of the city while Mardana entered the city. Mardana found it to be the land of gold. On enquiry he found the name of city to be Swaranpur ruled by king Kaul Nain, son of Surat Singh. Every one could eat whatever he wanted and there was no check. Order of the king was that every visitor will be given free food of his choice. Every item including the balance and weights in use, were of gold. A person known as Dharam Singh gave Mardana whatever he desired and asked him to take some sweet for his companions. Mardana however took nothing. On return, he told all the details about the city to Guru Nanak. Guru Nanak was happy that Mardana brought nothing. He told Mardana, "This is the city of Dharama. Hence, no one does any evil. Every one is contented. They do not have Turks in this state. They do not know Turks or even the idol worshippers."...Guru Nanak told the limits of the kingdom to be equal to nine thousand seven hundred yojan. No other king had such a vast territory in the world.

Mardana visited the city for 7 consequent days. Eighth day, Dharam Singh asked him about his companions, as to why they did not come. Mardana said, "They are contented. They live on air". Dharam Singh gave Mardana 2½ seer of sweets for him and 5 seers for Guru Nanak and Bala and reached alongwith Mardana the location where Guru Nanak was staying.

Anouncing his arrival with God's name, Dharam Singh presented the food. Guru Nanak refused to take it , stating, "Your king has done some wrong and he sould be knowing what it was." Dharam Singh was perplexed. He wanted to know what the wrong was but Guru Nanak refused to tell. Dharam Singh went to the king and stated what all happend. The king pondered over his entire past. Finding nothing wrong, he proceeded to Guru Nanak to clarify. Guru Nanak welcomed him and told him the details of his previous birth and the present life pointing out that he should not allow himself to be worshipped as he was not God. The king fell at Guru's feet and begged for forgiveness. Guru Nanak asked him to serve Sudharsain and rule over the area as a Dharam-Raja as he has been doing so far. Therefrom Guru Nanak proceeded to Sumer Parbat."[7]

Following islands/kingdoms/city-states and their rulers are found mentioned :-

Kingdom/City	King	Distance Travelled	Remarks
1. Bisihar	Sudharsain	15 days & nights journey form Bishambar-pur (Patna)	Jhanda-Badhi was established as preacher
2. Silmila Dweep and Behrampur	Madhurbain of Brahaman caste	Six months journey from Bishihar	
3. Deogandhar	Deoloot	Thirty Seven days and nights journey form Silmila Dweep	King was a cannibal.
4. PrasarNama City	Teekhan Tain	Three months journey from Deogandhar	Populated by apes. (or ape-like men)
5. Swaranpur	Kaulnain	Seven months thirteen days journey from Prasarnama City	(a) Gold in abundance (b) Free food for all (c) All of same caste (d) No Hindus, Muslims/Turks.

A total of 20 kings are found mentioned. These are 18 kings mentioned by Madhurbain i.e. Kavalnain, Madhurbain, Sudharsain, Sukhchain, Asrapan, Sagar Sen, BirMain, Lal Nain, Rai Ain, Sukh Sagar, Naga Paras Ram, Raja Atika -Ghatike, Sudh - Sambhalika, Budh - Bibek, - Balak, Raja Nain Jot, Raja Bali Singh, Raja Tutirang, and Raja Magan Rai, In addition, Raja Deoloot and Teekhantain are also mentioned.

Cannibalism existed in Deogandhar. Apes or ape like men lived on an island, Prasar Nama. Myth appears in the legend, as myth has been frequently added in Janamsakhi Bhai Bala.

The information given above has been studied in detail by various researchers and links have been established with the available facts. The details are as follows:-

(a) Both Dr. Trilochan Singh and Dr. Surinder Singh Kohli agree that Burma is recorded as Brahampur, and Swarandeep was actually Sondeep and part of Burma [7 and 8].

(b) Atka-Ghatka is the modified name of Chittagaon which was originally known as Chitta-Ghatka[10].

(c) Silmila Dweep has been indentified as Malaya Peninsula and includes, Siam, Annam, Cambodia, Java, Sumatra, Bali and Borneo.[11]

(d) 'Sudharsain is stated to be a powerful king of Chittagaon and Sondweep'.[12]

(e) Dr. Kohli also mentions, "It is said that there was a "Charan Padka" (the impression of the holy feet of the Guru) in Vat Sarkate (Temple) in Bangkok (Siam-Thailand). He is understood to have washed his hair at this place. He was held in profound veneration like Lord Buddha, therefore, the annual function at the temple is held on Kartik Purnima. Another temple in Bangkok known as Treyi Mitter (temple of three friends) is supposed to have been built in the memory of the Guru and his two companions, Bala and Mardana. It is also probable that the Guru visited Ayudhya also in Thailand, though the Ayudhya chronicles did not mentions Guru Nanak's visit to Thailand.[13]

(f) He further mentions, "If even the Guru touched China and Japan by this sea journey, we can assume that the Guru went to Peking and Nanking at this time. He was received respectfully by the king of China and the king and the people of China were so much impressed by the Guru that the city of Nanking was named in his honour."[14]

(g) Giani Lal Singh Sangrur also records in his account that Guru Nanak visited Assam, Kamkhya in Kamrup, Manipur, Lushai area of Burma, Syllhet, Ajmer Ganj, Karim Ganj and Ghargaon in Bangladesh, Rangoon and Mandley in Burma and Nanking and Peking in China. He also records, "At many places in China, Guru Nanak's idol is worshipped even now, and, he is remembered by the name of "Baba Bhusa"

(Fusang?) Due to lack of missionaries, places connected with Guru could not be preserved. Guru Nanak having discussions with Lama- Gurus in China blessed them with True Name. Many Jains and Buddhists became followers of Sikh religion."[15]

(h) There are places named Nanking (Zhuangsu Province), Nantong (Jiangsu Province), Nanjang (Henang Province), Nayang (Jianxi Province) and Nanping (Fujian Province) in China,[16] which similarly would have been named on Guru's name.

(j) Guru Nanak's Travel to Singapore is also recorded in the form of standing monument at Singapore.[17]

This researcher has been in the North East for about 10 years and from his knowledge finds that most likely Raja Bali was the king of Bali island and Naga Paras Ram was the king of Nagas in Nagaland, adjoining areas in Arunachal, Assam and Burma. Raja Turitarang was most likely the king of areas of Turriapani (Turfan) of Trans-Himalayan Region. Other kings seem to be small kings of Malaya Peninsula islands as according to Janamsakhi Bhai Bala, he visited all islands which were separated from each other and it took days to go from one island to another. To state that these were small kingdoms around Burma is not correct. For this purpose, detailed research is needed.

The researcher also interviewed, Ringdzin Rimpoche a Lama who was a professor of Tibetan in Vishav Bharati University and an authority on NyingMaPa Sect. He stated, "Guru Nanak visited Tibet extensively. He visited Mansarovar area again after he came to North Eastern Tibet from China visiting the famous lake of Kokonoor, the legend of which is attributed to Guru Nanak".

Taking all the above facts into account, it can be stated that Guru Nanak travelled widely into East Asia. Most likely, he visited some or all of the following countries in East Asia :- Bangladesh, Burma, Malaya, Indonesia, Bali, Thailand, Laos, Vietnam, China and Tibet.

The important places which appear to have been visited are as follows:-

Chittagaon, Rangoon, Mandley, (Both in Burma), Singapore, (Vat Sarkate) Bangkok, Ayudhia (Both in Thailand), NanPing (Zuangsu Province) Nanping (Fujian Province), Nanchang, (Jiangxi province) Nanking and Nantong (Jiangsu Province), Nanyang (Henang Province)

Nanchang, (Sichuan Province), and Kokonoor (North Eastern Tibet Autonomous Region) all in China. He either reached Kara-Koram Pass or alternatively on Mansarovar trail, visited Gartok, Rudok, Pansang Lake, Chushul and reached Ladakh. His journey into Ladakh and Kashmir is explained separately.

References

1. Surinder Singh Kohli : *Travels of Guru Nanak*, Chandigarh, Punjab University, 1978 (2nd edn) P.12.
2. Kirpal Singh (ed) : *Janam Sakhi Prampara*, Patiala, Punjabi University, 1969, P. 271.
3. Surinder Singh Kohli , Op. Cit. P.189-192.
4. Op. Cit. P.190.
5. Surinder Singh Kohli , Op. Cit P. 181-2.
6. Adopted from : *"Bale Wali Janam Sakhi"* in *Janamsakhi Prampara* edited by Kirpal Singh, P. 264-280.
7. Ibid
8. Surinder Singh Kohli (Dr) *Travels of Guru Nanak*, P.54.
9. Trilochan Singh (Dr.), *Jeevan Charit Guru Nanak Dev* P.165.
10. Ibid-
11. Surinder Singh Kohli (Dr.), P. 55-6.
12. Trilochan Singh (Dr.) P. 166.
13. Surinder Singh Kohli (Dr.) P. 56-7.
14. Ibid, P. 57.
15. Lal Singh Sangrur, (Giani), *Guru khalsa Twarikh*, P.70-1.
16. Arya, R.P.(ed), *The School Atlas*, P.25.
17. Joginder Singh Sahi, *'Sikh Shrines in India and Abroad*, P.137.

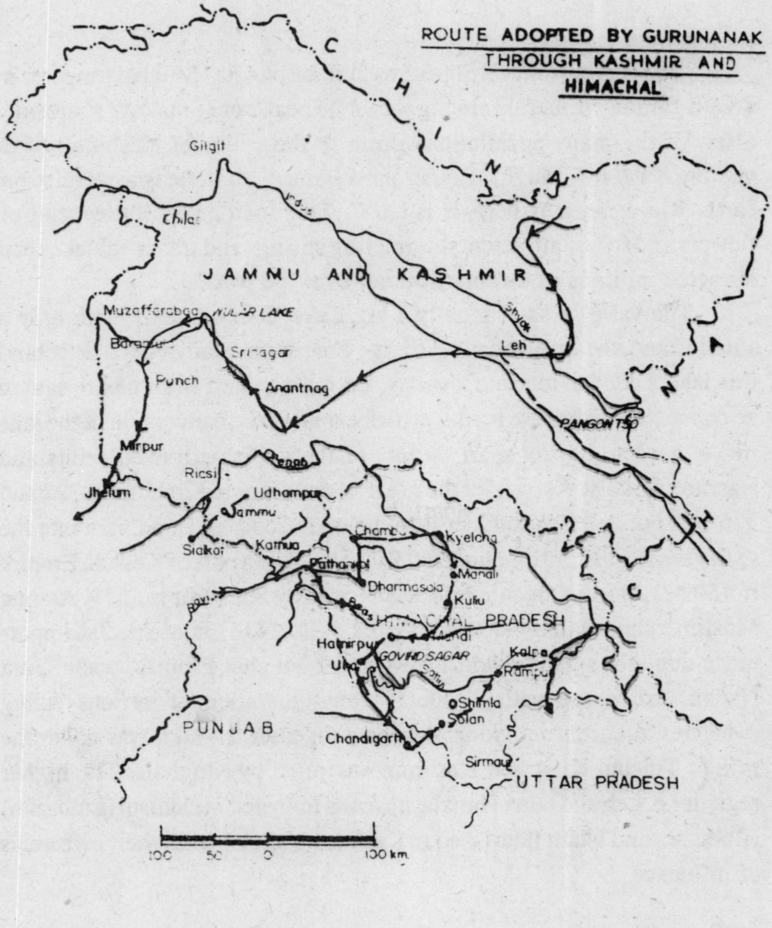
ROUTE ADOPTED BY GURUNANAK THROUGH KASHMIR AND HIMACHAL
CHINA
Gilgit
Indus
Chilas
JAMMU AND KASHMIR
Shyok
Muzaffarabad
WULAR LAKE
Srinagar
Leh
Punch
Anantnag
PANGON TSO
Mirpur
Chenab
Riasi
Jhelum
Udhampur
Jammu
Chamba
Kyelang
Sialkot
Kathua
Pathankot
Manali
Dharmasala
Kullu
Ravi
Beas
HIMACHAL PRADESH
Mandi
Hamirpur
GOVIND SAGAR
Kalpa
Una
Satluj
Rampur
Shimla
Solan
PUNJAB
Chandigarh
Sirmaur
UTTAR PRADESH
100
50
0
100 km.

Kashmir

'The Happy Valley' "Super Switzerland of Asia" Mughal Emperor's dream garden' "Emerald among the white pearls of Himalaya's" are only a few of the many appellations given to the valley of Kashmir. After visiting Kashmir, Mughal Emperor exclaimed, "If there is a paradise on earth, it is here, it is here, it is here". This lush green Valley, full of flowers and fruits, attractive shimmering springs and traslicent lakes had attracted millions of visitors from all over the world.

The valley was originally a big Lake 'Satisar Lake' with only a small island, the tip of today's, Takht-i-Suleiman. Many myths lie behind this lake's conversion into a valley. Lord Shiva and Brahma are said to be connected with these myths, which explains the conversion of the lake into a garden. Myths apart, beauty of the valley, attracted saints and warriors equally. Alexander the great advanced onto Kashmir in 327 and 326 BC, but failed to conquer it. Ashoka, introduced Buddhism into the valley during his rule, around 250 BC. it became a part of Kushan Empire in 150 AD. During Muslim rule, it was ruled by Shah Mir in 1339. Among Muslim rulers Zain-Ul-Abidi (around A.D. 1413) is of special importance due to his good work. It was under Mughal Empire, when Guru Nanak visited the valley. Due to conglomeration of various ruling dynasties, different religions prospered together. Ladakh was under the rule of Tibetan King and Kashmir was ruled by Mughals. The higher regions i.e. Leh and other Himalayan tracts followed Buddhism (Lamasim) Hinduism and Islam flourished in Kashmir Valley within their own areas of influence.

Leh

'Guru Nanak entered Jammu & Kashmir State from Kashgar and Yarkand' (China) through Karakoram Pass and reached Leh,[1] as per Dr. Kohli, however Drs. Fauja Singh and Kirpal Singh mention Guru Nanak reaching Leh through Chushul after visit of Mansarovar.[2] The second route seems more plausible. There is a tree near Leh under which Guru Nanak sat and delivered sermons. The tree is treated to be sacred by the local people.

Basgo

From Leh Guruji visited number of places in Ladakh. At a distance of 24 k.m. to the West of Leh on Leh-Kargil road in the village Basgo. There is a rock on the roadside about 8 feet high and 8 feet in diameter. It has a cavity which appears to have the impressions of head, shoulders and upper part of the body of man.

"Legend has it that a few hundred years ago when Nanak Shah was returning from Yarkand he halted there for sometime. His fame had spread far and wide. Becoming jealous of Nanak Shah's great virtues, a local demon or some other faquir rolled down the huge boulder from a hill to kill Nanak Shah. But by a miracle, the stone became plastic like wax and enveloped the body of the saint. Nanak Shah walked out of it unhurt and unscathed leaving a deep impression in the stone[3]. Recently a Gurudwara has been constructed near the place to commemmorate the event. (For more details see interview with Lt Col H.S. Bakshi attached as appendix F.)

Karu

Guru Nanak also visited Karu. 'There are two small hutments near Karu, where the people worship only Guru Nanak and no other God.[4] It shows the impact of Guru's visit to the place, however, no Gurdwara has yet been constructed there.

Hemus Gompha

Guru Nanak also visited Hemus Gompha, 40 k.m. south of Leh where he held discussions with Lamas. Many people in Hemus believe that foundation stone of the Hemus Gompha was laid by Guru Nanak himself[5].

Skardu

From Leh, passing through Karu and Hemus, he moved towards Skardu. The Guru passed through Nimu and Khaltse and reached Skardu. 'There used to be an ancient Gurdwara before 1949, however, its present state is not known[6].

There used to be an old route from Skardu to Kargil. Going on this route towards south, Guru Nanak reached Kargil. There is a historical Gurdwara in memory of Guru's visit, very close to a temple. This shows that the Guru came face-to-face with pandits and held discussions.

Amarnath

"From Kargil the Guru proceeded to the famous Zozila pass which is about 80 k.m. to the south. He stayed at Drasnagar near Zozila."[7] Therefrom Guruji proceeded to the famous religious centre Amarnath, the place of Lord Shiva[8]. A Shivilinga formed by the drops of trickling water is the chief attraction and worship. From Amarnath Guruji proceeded to Mattan.

Mattan

At Mattan Guru Nanak met Kamal-ud-din and Braham Das, a Muslim saint and Pandit of the area. 'Kamal-ud-din and Braham Prakash, though grown aged at the time of Guru Nanak's arrival in Mattan, were friends right from their childhood days'[9]. They both were of the same age as well as class mates in the same maqtab. They belonged to the two leading families of Mattan which were deeply religious and claimed well-known uleman and pandits among their ancestors.

'Kamal-ud-din's father was the Chief Quazi at Srinagar and had held other high offices in the state. Braham Das's father was a well known scholar and the chief priest at the local temple. He owned a large farm and a couple of orchards.

After the maktab, Kamal-ud-din went to madrasa and studied Persian, Arabic and the Quaran and Islamic Jurisprudence. He got interested in becoming a Qazi or a priest for which he was given special training. He went to Afghanistan, Persia and Iraq, the famous centres of

Islamic learning, for further studies and went to Mecca on Hajj. On returing he was appointed the Chief Imam of important histoical mosques. After retiring from the state service, he returned to his ancestoral village of Mattan.

Kamal-ud-din had towering personality. He was over six feet tall, and had bold, prominant features, a pepper and salt flowing beard and thick, glossy haircut behind at the base of his neck. He was a proud and temperamental man with anger writ large in his eyes. A fierce fire burnt within him which made him out of control of himself at slightest provocation. He could not stand contradiction or criticism. He often lost his job because he could not control his anger, He married thrice and had a number of children and grandchildren. Despite his faults, he was a deeply religious man. He prayed five times a day, observed Ramzan fasts vigorously and gave away tenth of his earning as charity. However, he missed the peace and contentment he longed for.[10]

Brahm Das, after his days at Maktab, studied Prakrit and Sanskrit at home under a tutor. Later for higher studies, he went to Benaras. He was an astute schloar of Sanskrit and studied all the ancient scriptures diligently. He was gifted with a phenomenal memory and could quote verse and chapter from ancient scriptures with an ease that astounded his audience. He became a well known grammarian and earned considerable respect at most of the Hindu places of learning. He had a mania for books and, in course of time, could claim a fine library of his own. He taught for short intervals at several centres of learning and acted as priest at famous temples. But he was essentially a scholar and, early in life retuned to Mattan and pursued his religious studies. He came to be known for some of the commentaries, he had written on ancient scriptures.

Brahm Dass was a handsome Kashmiri Brahmin of medium height with exquisitely fine features. Everything was so well proportioned about him that he looked like a model for sculptors. He had long capering hands of an artist, strangely pale blue eyes and a thick mop of hair which he frequently parted with his left hand. He was usually dressed in a white shirt (Kurta) and a white chooridar kurta being embroidered with designs in needle works. He was married but had no children. His home was a veritable Mecca for scholars and academicians. If, however, he was obliged to visit any sage or scholar, he carried his books on camels, the loads he kept ready for ready reference. He had one more oddity; he had an exquisitely carved idol which he hung round his neck with a silver chain. It was a tiny idol of his favourite deity.[10]

In Mattan, Guru Nanak found a resting place, near a fountain surrounded by a small orchard of apple and almond trees. Today the fountain has taken the shape of the tank with hundreds of fish floating in it. There is a row of rooms beind this tank and one of the rooms has been turned into a Gurdwara in memory of Guru Nanak"[11].

Mattan is the town of pandits. Dozen of them crowd around every bus that brings visitors to their place. The unusual dress of Guru Nanak too would have attracted quite a few brahmins around him and naturally many questions would have been addressed to him about his faith and beliefs. It being the season of pigrimage to Amarnath, the visitors too started thronging in numbers towards Guru Nanak. Most people came out of curiousity about the Guru's magnetic personality, his captivating sermons and the mystrical texture of his hymns that aroused their interest and made them come more than once. When Kamal-ud-din heard about Guru's sermons and their popularity among the people, he was curious but disturbed. That Guru Nanak preaching about the One/only as a prophet or messenger of God and as a medium between men and God' was considered highly dangerous by Kamal-ud-din who regarded himself as both the protector and guide of the Muslims of mattan. He decided to go and see for imself what kind of a man was the new saint.[10]

Kamal-ud-din, followed by two attendants, went to the orchard with a fountain, where Guru Nanak was having a lively discussion with a few pandits. When the pandits noticed the arrival of Kamal-ud-din, they stood up and bowed to him. Guru Nanak too, invited him with courtesy, as was his nature and asked him to sit near him.

"Are you bound for Amarnath yatra?" enquired Kamal

"No"

"Then, to where?"

"Wherever God directs".

"To whom are you to meet?"

"Whosoever he wants me to meet"

"How do you know that ?"

"He guides himself"

Kamal-ud-din looked at Guru Nanak carefully. He felt the depth of the answers. With some hesitation, he said, "You do not worship idols; you worship the God alone?".

"Yes, the one and the only God, the Supreme Reality".

"That is indeed as it should be", "said Kamal-ud-din, "But what about the Prophet—Prophet Mohammed?".

"I seek to establish a direct link with The God". replied Guru Nanak.

Kamal raised his head and said, "May be, it is possible for you but we need the help of the Prophet".

"Use it by all means, But in the end; you have to travel yourself".

"I pray five times a day for the support of the final journey".

"But there are two things, Sheikh Kamal-ud-din; one; the daily prayers of God should not be mere recitations, two: have a feeling that it is very difficult to be a true Mussalman".

"You speak in riddles Baba Nanak. Pray speak more directly" murmured Kamal-ud-din.

Guru Nanak recited the following Hymn;

(Panj Niwaja Wakhat Panj; Majh Var I) [12]

"There are five prayers and five times
And all the five have their names,
The first, is truth,
The second, right occupation
The third, charity in the name of God,
The fourth, is right resolve
And fifth, the praise of God.
Recite the kalma of righteous deeds
And then call yourself a Mussalman".

"Subhan Allah, Subhan Allah, shouted Kamal-ud-din "Pray tell me, how can one become a true Muslim?" Guru ji then recited:-

(Muslman Kahavan Muskal: Majh Var 1)[13].

"Difficult it is to claim to be a Muslim,
To do so one must live and act like a Muslim.

First he must be devoted to faith in God and the Prophet,
And remove all pride and vanity of wealth
Through charity, as the fire, removes the rust.
After becoming a Muslim, one should abide by Islam".
"How to achieve this standard"?. Asked Kamal-ud-din
Guru Nanak recited another Shabd:-

"Mihir Masit Sidak Mussalla—Majh Var 1) [14]

"If compassion be the mosque and the prayer mat,
And honest living one's Quran;
And humility one's circumcision and continuance one's fasting
Then verily, one may be called a Musalman.
If virtuous deed make one's pilgrimage to Kaaba,
And truth be the guide of one's spirit.
And prayer be the Lord's grace
and the rosary be of His Will.
Then God will assuredly keep one's honour".

Kamal-ud-din was thrilled by the thought that to be a Musalman, one needed compassions, faith, honest living, humility, continuance, virtuous deeds, truth, a rosary of God's will and prayer for His Grace. Moreover he needs the love of religions, a clean heart, acceptance of God's will, annihilation of the ego and compassion for all living beings.

After the discussions, Kamal-ud-din sat with a bowed head. He looked into his own heart and felt imperfect and empty before the Guru. A faint hope stirred in him Trembling with emotions, he said, "What hope is there for me Baba Nanak? A fire burns in my heart which restricts my upward flight. I am afflicted with anger, how can I overcome it?".

"It is your ego Kamal-ud-din. Tear from your heart too much of your wisdom, power, position, influence, even your physical strength. Think of all the mighty ones who have been consigned to the dark silence of the grave. Go down before the lord on your knees and wash your sins with your tears. Humility is the answer to your application".

Kamal-ud-din touched Guru Nanak's feet and walked as though in a dream. Suddenly, like a flash of lighting, he realised the cause as well as the cure for his malady and brought a tremendous change in his outlook of life. He visited Guru Nanak daily and listened to his words with utmost devotion.

Some days later, Kamal went to share his experience with age-old friend Braham Das.

Braham Das was a keen observer of men. As soon as Kamal entered his room, he noticed the change in his friend. The hauteur, the arrogant looks, the chin up and the chest out and above all, the thundering voice were all missing. He looked wasted out and very mush subdued.

"Welcome my friend", he said with mock hilarity, "I hope the ladies at home have not turned you out?".

"It is not the time for jokes Brahm Das. I came to find out if you have been to see the new sanyasi who has come to our town. If not, you had better done that".

"Is this a friendly advice or you want to make a fool of myself? What have I to learn from such wandering Yogi who sings his own hymns?"

"He is a rare type. Dont's miss the opportunity or you will regret".

"Are you serious about it?" enquired Brahm Dass.

"Yes in all seriousness. No more questions. Do as I direct".

Kamal went back leaving Brahm Dass agitated and restless. He felt that for a scholar of his standing, it was unbecoming to pay homage to a wandering Sadhu, Yet he could not ignore the advice of Kamal-ud-din. With great reluctance, he plannned to go to Guru Nanak.

'Pandit Brahm Dass loaded his books on two camels and assisted by his attendants went to Guru Nanak[15]. The attendants went ahead and announced, "The Pandit of Mattan has come to see you." Guru Nanak said, "It is a great honour. He is most welcome".

Brahm Dass entered with his camels, and walked with all his dignity and with a slight bow of his head, greeted the Guru. Guru Nanak received him with folded hands and said, "You are welcome Pandit Brahm Dass. It deems an honour to receive you. I have learnt about your scholarship but why bring these books on camels"?.

But Brahm Dass seeing at Guru Nanak's disposition asked a volley of questions, "What type of a saint are you? why are you wearing these skins? Why have you tied the rope around you? Why have you left the normal way of life"?[16].

The Guru listened to him calmly and replied "There is no need of any worldly posture to worship him and no rituals are required for His Name; Because He is the maker of the entire universe." Guru Nanak recited a Shabd:-

(Apine aap saaj aap pachhania: (Var Malhar Ki, Mahila 1)[17]

He created the universe; He alone knows its essence;
He separated sky and earth; and created a canopy;
Erecting the sky without pillers is the example of his power.
He gave his light to Sun and Moon.
He creates days and nights which is another great wonder;
The elders believe in ritual baths and discussion on religion.
But there is no one equal to God; This everyone says.
True is the abode in Him; rest all is transitory". (SGGS : 1279)

Braham Dass was non-plussed.

"Any more question you wish to ask, please do so," asked Guru Nanak.

Braham Dass was spell bound. Then Guru Nanak repeated his question "What was the need of two camel load of books' 'I thought you might ask some questions?' replied Braham Dass "But I have none to ask", Braham Dass was astonished at the Guru's answer. He was a born debater. He loved to argue, ask questions and find faults and quote authority to impress and denounce his opponents.

"I am surprised that you have no curiosity, no inquistiveness and no desire to gain more knowledge. Well that was your affair. If you have no question, may I ask you a few more?" said Braham Das.

"You may, but remember, that my answers will be simple because my faith is simple and unburdened with complexities".

"How simple? Is it not based on any of the six schools of philosophy?"

"No", replied Guru Nanak, "It is simple because it is exclusively based on the love of God and His people".

"Well that's interesting; what deities do you worship? Rama, Krishna, Shiva or Vishnu?"

"None of these. I worship One and the only One, The God".

"How do you define Him? " Guru Nanak replied.

(Ik Onkar.....Mul Mantra, Japuji Sahib)[18]

'God, almighy Lord, is one alone,
All-Pervading,
Eternal source of all universe,
Self-existent, unborn too,
He knoweth no fear nor wrath, Cherishes ill to none,
Above the pains of birth and death Beyond transmigration;
By divine grace, Worship Him always'.

Brahm Dass was impressed as every word touched the core of his heart, but still he wanted to know more, "Any thing more"? he requested.

The Guru further recited:- *(Ad Sach, Jugad Sach—Japji)*[20]

Existance true who doth abide
Since times unknown
Primal ages and past absure
Days dead and gone
In the living present as well
Doth live the Deity
And in the endless future too
The Lord shall be.

Brahm Dass tried to comprehend the concept of God as Truth. All the same, he said, "Hail?'

Guru Nanak recited:-

(The One Supreme Lord is Unique, He is Immortal, Unborn without Involvement. He is Unfathomable, beyond the reach of senses, without form or lives. Searching for Him, I found Him in my heart' (Bilawal Tith-I) (SGGS P. 832) Braham Dass nodded his head and said, "I, too, believe in the Supreme Lord but one needs an image or an idol as a symbol to direct his devotion".

In reply Guru Nanak recited a hymn :-

Supreme Order of Providence
Which baffles all eloquence
Created the whole universe,
And each thing in existence,
By his order all honour comes,

Pain, pleasure, weal or woe,
One might beg or wear a crown
Beings are born high or low.
The supreme order swayeth all,
And beyond its pale none abide,
whoever bends before His word,
Shall shine free of vain, pride."
"Who is He and who has created Him?" asked Brahm Dass.
The Guru replied (Thapia na jai kita na hoi: Japji)
"He cannot be proved, for he is uncreated;
He is without matter, self-existent.
They that serve shall honoured be,
'O' Nanak! the Lord is most excellent
Praise the Lord, hear them that do Him praise,
In your hearts His name be graven,
Sorrows from your soul erase
And make your hearts a joyous haven.
The Guru's word has the sages' wisdom,
The Guru's word is full of learning,
For though it be the Guru's word
God Himself speaks therein
Thus run the words of the Guru
God is the Destroyer, Preserver and Creator
God is the Goddess too.
Words to describe are hard to find.
I would venture if I knew.'
This alone my teacher taught
There is but one Lord of all creation
Forget Him not."

"What was existent before this universe" Braham Dass enquired further. Guru Nanak answered :-

(Arbad Narbad Dhudukara — Maru Sohila Mahila 1)

'For countless ages, there was utter darkness. there was no earth and no sky, but the Infinite Lord's Will alone was pervasive. There was neither day, nor night, nor moon, nor sun, but the

Lord alone sat in profound grace. Neither there were mines of creation, nor speech, nor air, nor water. Neither creation, nor destruction, nor coming, nor going. There were no continents, nor under-worlds nor seven oceans, nor rivers nor the flowing of water. There was no higher, middle and lower plane. Neither there was hell, nor heaven, nor death, nor time. There was no world of torture or reign of bliss, no birth nor death; nor did anyone come or go. There was no Brahma nor Vishnu nor Shiva. None else was seen but He, the One Lord. Neither was there any female, nor male, nor caste, nor did any one suffer pain or pleasure. There was neither the celibate, nor the man of charity nor the forest-dweller. There was no adept, no striver, no dweller at ease. There was no yogi, wandering sage in the religious garb and none called himself the supreme yogi. There was no contemplation, penance, self-control, fasting and worship. Nor did anyone speak or tell of quality. Creating His ownself, the Lord was supremely rejoined and Himself valued His ownself. There was no purifications, or self restraint, or rosary of sweet basil. There was no milk-maid. There were no incantations and spells, no hypocrisy, nor did any one play on the flute. There were no deeds, religion and the gadfly of mammon. Caste and birth differences did not exist. There was no noose of secular attachment, nor was death writ on the moral's brow. There was no slander, no seed, no soul and no life".

'Braham Dass was visibly impressed. He threw the idol away and ordered the beeds to be burnt. He became Guru Nanak's follower instantly and zealously. He became proud of Guru's service which Guru did not approve. Guru Nanak asked him, "Go, find some other Guru". 'Braham Dass wanted to know whom should he contact. The Guru replied, "Go to the garden.There is a house near by where you will find four saints sitting there. They will guide you further." Braham Dass did as directed. The saints asked him to go to the adjoining that temple. Braham Dass reached the temple. There he found a beautiful woman in red attire. whom he approached she got furious at being disturbed and beat him with chains very severely. Crying, Braham Dass reached the four saints again and explained them what all happened. The saints replied, "That was Maya.

Your ego is materialistic and your Guru has been the same 'Maya'. Go back again to Guru Nanak. He alone is the perfect guide." Braham Dass came running to Guru Nanak and followed him with true spirit and without pride. Guru Nanak recited a hymn at seeing the condition of Braham Dass. (Sahansar dan de inder Rowaia)[22].

> 'With the award of the punishment of the thousand marks of valva, Inder did weep. Paras Ram came home crying. Ajai waited, when made to eat the dung he gave in charity. Such is the punishment meted out in God's court. Rama wept when he was exiled and got separated from Sita and Lakshaman. Ten headed Ravana, who took away Sita with the beat of Tumbourine, wept, when he lost Lanka. The Pandavs, whose wife, Draupadi was lost to Kauravs became their servant and wailed. Janmeja too wailed when he went astray and for an offence he became a sinner. The divine teachers, seers and religious guides weep, lest they should suffer agony at the last moment. The kings weep, having their ears torn and go begging from house to house. The miser weeps when his amassed wealth parts company with him. The learned man cries when his learning fails him. The young woman weeps for she has no husband. Nanak says, the whole world is in distress. He, who believes in the Name, becomes victorious. No other deed is of any account".

Guru Nanak redeemed him finally. Pandit Braham Dass became the exponent of Guruvani. 'A gurdwara was constructed at the place where Guru Nanak was seated and delivered sermons. During Maharaja Ranjit Singh's time, continuous recitation of six Akhand Paths was in progress, The original Dharamsala has now fallen and the Guru Granth Sahib is placed in a new room[23].

From Mattan Guru Nanak proceeded to Srinagar about 64 k.m. to the south through Anantnag. There is a Shankarcharya Temple visible from the city itself. 'While staying there Guru Nanak met number of yogis. They too were redeemed like Braham Dass. A Gurdwara was constructed at Hariparbat in honour of Guru Nanak's visit to this place[24].

From Srinagar, Guru Nanak proceeded to Baramulla. The city is about 56 k.m. from Srinagar. 'A Gurdwara Harmukh Ganga on the bank of Jhelum is in the memory of Guru Nanak. He proceeded to Uri, about 20 k.m. from Baramulla and reached Kohala[25].

About 48 k.m. from Kohala and 8 k.m. from the main road, there is a Gurdwara Kalyansar, the place visited by Guru Nanak from Kohala. Therefrom the Guru turned towards Punjab.

References

1. Surinder Singh Kohli (Dr), *Travels of Guru Nanak,* P.128.
2. Fauja Singh Kirpal Singh (Drs), *Atlas Travels of Guru Nanak,* P.30.
3. K.M. Vaid, *Hindustan Times;* October 25, 1969.
4. Kirpal Singh Dr (Ed), *Janam Sakhi Prampra,* P.107.
(Record of Statement of Col.J.S. Gularia).
5. Kirpal Singh Dr (Ed), *Janam Sakhi Prampara,* P.107.
6. Kahan Singh Nabha (Bhai) ; *Mahankosh:* Under para heading *'Mattan Sahib'*
7. Balwant Singh, *Guru Nanak, Guru Nanak Foundation,* New Delhi 1983, P.158.
8. Ibid.
9. Ibid.
10. Ibid, P.159 to 162.
11. Kahan Singh Nabha (Bhai), *Mahankosh,* under para heading *'Mattan Sahib'.*
12. *Sri Guru Granth Sahib,* P.141.
13. Ibid.
14. Ibid, P.140.
15. *Puratan Janam Sakhi,* P.18.
16. Kirpal Singh Dr. (Ed) : *JanamSakhi Prampara,* P.109.
17. *Sri Guru Granth Sahib,* P.1279.
18. *Sri Guru Granth Sahib,* P.1.
19. *Ibid.*
20. Op. Cit P.4.
21. *Sri Guru Granth Sahib,* P.953.
22. Kahan Singh Nabha (Bahri), *Mahan Kosh* : See Word "Kashmir'
23. Ibid.
24. Kahan Singh Nabha - *Mahan Kosh* : See Word 'Kashmir'

Return to Punjab

In those days three routes were used from Kashmir to reach West Punjab Kartarpur. These were :-

1. Srinagar, Birhamgalla, Rajouri, Naushera, Bhimber, Gujrat/ Wazirabad, Sialkot, Kartarpur. Sikh Army won Kashmir by this route.

2. Srinagar, Birhamgala, Rajouri, Chingus, Naushera, Peer Satwan, Quila Khamas, Jhellum, Sialkot, Kartarpur.

3. Srinagar, Baramula, Kohala, Kaliansar, Hassan Abdal (Punja Sahib) Sialkot, Kartarpur. There are numerous Gurdwaras on this route, commemorating Guruji's visit, hence it is most likely that Guruji adopted this route.

Hasan Abdal

Guruji proceeded to Hassan Abdal through Attock. Attock was originally a Budhist centre. Remains of viharas and stupas can still be seen on adjoining hills.

The village was established around a dharamsala constructed by a Gujjar named Hassan. 'Name Hassan Abdal is said to be originated from the name Hassan itself'[1].

Guru Nanak is said to have met Hassan while he was looking after his pet animals. He presented milk to Guruji, which was taken both by Guruji and Mardana"[2]. 'Hassan's grave is still existent near the hill.'

A Muslim saint (faqir) named 'Wali Kandhari' used to stay on a nearby hill. "He belonged to Rafzi sect of Shias. His original name was Yar Ali'[3]. He met Guruji and held discussions as follows:-

'Yar Ali, "What is your name"?

Guru Nanak "My name is Nanak Nirankari"

Yar Ali, "Whose follower are you?"

Guru Nanak, "I am God's man".

Yar Ali "Is your God alive or dead?"

Guru Nanak, "My God is everyone's God and is ever living".

Yar Ali "How can one reach him?

Guru Nanak: "He is everywhere. You just have to remember and He will listen to you".

Guru Nanak told him about God's True Existence.

(Yak Arz Guftam pes to dar peas kum Kartar, Haka Kabir Karim Tun Beaib Pervardgar,[4]) *(Tilang Mahila 1 SGGS,* P. 722)

'I utter, one supplication before thee. Hear it thou 'O' my Creator. You are the true, great, merciful and faultless cherisher.

The world is perishable, know it for certain in thy mind. Azrail, deaths's courier, has caught me by the hair of head? Yet I know it not in the least in my heart, thy wife. When I fail and the time of last prayer comes, there shall be no one to rescue me. Night and day, I wander in avarice and think of and do evil. I do not, ever do good deeds, I am unfortunate as also miserly, negligent, shameless and without Thine fear, O Lord. Says Nanak, I am Thy slave and the dust of the feet of Thine servants.

Yar Ali was satisfied and became Guruji's follower. Another story connected with Yar Ali which had been in current goes as follows, "Guru Nanak and Mardana came to rest near the foot of a hill on which Wali Kandhari lived. Mardana felt thirsty and looked around for water. There was no water to be found anywhere. He suddenly noticed the hut on top of the hill and decided to go up and see if he could get some water there. Under the blazing midday sun, going up the hill was no easy task. Mardana had to climb mostly on his hand and kness as the stones were slippery. Panting and puffing, he went up to Wali Kandhari and requested for water'[5].

Wali Kandhari looked up and said "Who are you and what brings you here?"

"I and my master are on our way to Kartarpur. I felt thirsty, As there was no water any where near, I came upto see if you could help me."

"Your Master? Who is he?"

"Guru Nanak. A man of God, a prophet, a noble soul".

"A prophet, you said? Go and get water from him. I have nothing for you".

Mardana returned deeply disappointed and narrated all this to Guruji. Guru Nanak said, “You must not have displayed enough humility. Remember! we faqirs have three weapons; meekness, humility and sweet words. Go back and humbly request for water.” Mardana gathered strength and went up the hill perspiring. “You are back again?”

"Salaam-a Lekum: My master sends you greetings and requests for some water for me", Mardana bowed and said softly. "Go away and ask your master to find you water. I cannot understand how a Muslim can accept a Hindu as his peer. You are an apostate and can expect no mercy from me." Dejected and depressed, Mardana returned to Guru Nanak and told what had happened again.

Guruji asked Mardana to remove a stone from the slope of the hill. Lo! a stream of fresh water gushed down. Mardana had his fill. Suddenly, Wali Kandhari realised the water in his tank reducing speedily. He looked down the hill and found Mardana enjoying the water and Guru Nanak and Bala sitting nearby.

In rage, he threw a large boulder on them. Guruji saw the boulder coming down roaring. As it came down, Guru Nanak raised his hands and the stone rested there itself. Marks of Guruji's hand are imprinted on the stone for ever. A magnificant Gurdwara, known as Panja Sahib has been built at the place. The stone, with the imprint of Guruji's hand (Panja) forms part of the pool adjacent to the Gurdwara. The town of Hassan Abdal is now called Panja Sahib.

Wali Kandhari came down the hill and fell at Guru Nanak's feet and asked for forgiveness. Guru Nanak told him that love is the one and the only thing by which one can win over God and His people.

Guru Nanak stayed at Hassan Abdal for some days and then proceeded towards Kartarpur on the main road Peshawar-Lahore constructed by Sher Shah Suri”.

Tilla Bal Gudain

Guru Nanak reached Tilla Bal Gudain (Now district Jhellum). The place is called Tilla Bal Gudain because a woman, to test a yogi, tied up his hair. This place of yogis was 24 km to North West of Jhellum. In Aeen-e-Akbari, mention of this place is made as follows', “In the Doab of Sindh Sagar, there is a place of Bal Nath Yogi near Shamshabad. The place is called Tilla Bal Nath. Yogis come to visit from far and near'[6].

Guru Nanak came and relaxed near Bal Nath Ashram. 'The saint when he came to know about Guruji's presence conducted Guruji to his place personally'[7].

With great affection, he held discussion with Guruji. His questions included "Who is your Guru? What is the method of your salvation? etc."

Guru Nanak sang in ecstasy;

Ham dolat Bedi Pap Bhari hai (*Ramkali Mahila 1, SGGS*, P. 878)

My boat filled with sin dwindles even with the blow of wind. Saints and Siddhs have come to discuss; You must give them importance.
'O' God ! You must save me by becoming my guide
'O' The absolute and Omnipresent; give me the boon.
'Of your Name; I am ever grateful to you.
Siddhs and Yogis all worship Thy Name.
They move bare feet once they come to know about Your Name.
Repetition of Your Name, meditation and application
Are not known to me; I only take Your Name.
God himself is my Guru, who has given me the true hymns for salvation."

Bal Nath was impressed at this. He became a follower and friend of Guru Nanak. Guru Nanak stayed with him for some days. 'The place where the Guru was seated, has footmarks of Guruji. There was a small Gurdwara built to commemorate the memory of the event. A pujari used to look after this place till the origin of Pakistan'[8].

'Near this place, the famous fort of Rohtas is situated. This was built by Sher Shah Suri after Guru's visit. The name of the city inside the fort is also known as Rohtas'[9]. Also there used to be a spring near the fort, which was called as Choha Baba Nanak. 'This spring is said to commemorate Guru's visit, as this was originated by the Guru by removing a stone'[9].

From Tilla Bal Gudain, the Guru travelled on the route what was later known as Sher Shah Suri Marg. Crossing Jhellum and Chenab; he reached Sialkot which was an ancient town. 'Its name was Sialkot and had the honour of being the capital of ancient Punjab'[10].

Sialkot

On reaching Sialkot Guru Nanak, alongwith his companions sat under a mulbery (ber) tree. There is a Gurdwara at this place now, The travellers before partition used to pay homage to the place. From here, the Guru sent Bhai Mardana to the city to buy falsehood and truth for one paisa each. Mardana went to all the shops, but no one entertained him. A shopkeeper named Moola wrote on a slip. 'Truth is that every one dies and False is to say that every one forever'. Mardana took the slip and reached the Guru. Guru Nanak was very much impressed by the reply and met Mula at his shop. He told Bhai Mula, "You have the knowledge of the fact of life as you have differentiated between truth and falsehood". Bhai Moola was pleased. He said "If I have something incomplete still it shall be complete with your guidance". The Guru held discussions with Bhai Mula, who in turn impressed by the Guru left his home and hearth and moved alongwith. After staying for a few days, Guruji proceeded towards Talwandi.

Kotla Mian Mitha

From Sialkot, the Guru alongwith Bhai Bala, Bhai Mardana and Bhai Moola reached Kotla Mian Mitha near Pasrur and stayed in a garden, a kilometer outside the city. When Mian Mitha came to know about Guru's arrival, he spoke to his followers, "Nanak has come to our town. He is a God-gifted saint. If we meet him, he will redeem us like fresh butter taken out of milk". Guru Nanak came to know of it. He spoke to Mardana, If we meet Mitha, I will squeeze his sins like a lemon". Mian Mitha soon reached the Guru He bowed to Guru Nanak and said.[11]

"First of all appeared the Name of God; then of Nabi Rasool. If you read his scriptures, you will be accepted in God's court'.

Guru Nanak replied, "First of all appeared the Name of God. Rasool turned out to be his gateman. You must correct your vision, 'O' Sheikh; then only you will be accepted in God's court".

Mian Mitha questioned "Is there a possibility to burn a lamp without oil?"

The Guru replied, *"Achall Chhalai Nah gha Chhalai Nah Kataran Kar Sakai"*[12] (Sri Rag SGGS P. 25)

"In this body-lamp put the oil of the practice of reciting the religious books and the wick of Lord's fear. Light this lamp with the fire of the knowledge of truthfulness. With this oil shall thy lamp burn. Make such light and then, shalt thou meet the Lord. When Guru's words soften this body-soul and service is performed, happiness is obtained. All the world continues coming and going. In this world only Lord is permanent. Get his blessings, then shalt thou get a seat in the Master's court and swing thy arm happily". Thereafter Mian Mitha had a volley of questions. 'Guruji, please tell me the reading from Quran which shall make me accepted by Him?" the Guru replied.

Mihir Masit Sidaq Mussalla (SGGS P. 140)

'If compassion be the mosque and the prayer be thy mate
And honest living one's Quaran;
circumcision and continence one's
fasting; Then verily, one may be called a Musslman.
If virtuous deed one's pilgrimage to Ka'aba
And truth be the guide of one's spirits
And prayer be the Lord's grace.
And the rosary of His Will
Then God will assuredly keep one's honour'.

Mian Mitha was very much impressed by Guru's words. He paid him obeissance. After staying for a few days with him, Guruji proceeded to Talwandi.

Talwandi

Alongwith Bhai Bala, Bhai Mardana and Bhai Moola, Guru Nanak reached Talwandi and sat down outside the village. Mardana went and met his family. When Guru Nanak's parents came to know about his return, they went and brought him home. Entire family members got together. Return of Guru Nanak after a long period, created happiness amongst all. Father was very eager to give all sorts of delicious food and sweets, but Guruji had crossed all tastes; hence he said.

'Sabh ras mithei Manien, suniain salone: (Sri Rag Mahila 1 SGGS, P. 16)

> All the tastes may be sweet; though heard as sour. The spoken words may be killing. With His blessings' even thirty six types of amrits will give one taste of His Name. 'O', old man! every food except on God's Name is useless; what is the use of taking such food which creates pains and produces evil in mind.

The Guru stayed at Talwandi for some days. Moola returned to Sialkot while Guruji alongwith Bala and Mardana proceeded to Sultanpur.

Sutanpur

At Sultanpur, Guru Nanak met his family and sister Nanki and brother-in-law Jai Ram. Daulat Khan Lodhi was at Sultanpur at that time. He was made Subedar of Punjab by Sikandar Lodhi, hence he stayed usually at Lahore and visited Sultanpur occasionally. When he came to know about Guru Nanak's arrival in Sultanpur he met Guruji. He enquired about Guru Nanak's place of residence. Guruji recited a hymn.

Mukam kar ghar baisna, Nit Chalne ke dholeh (Sri Rag Mahila 1 SGGS P. 64)

> 'What is the use of settling in such a place for residence: wherefrom there is always fear of departure; Residence should be of permanent nature. What type of residence is this world? You must have faith in Lord. Spend only what you earn; and get attached to God's Name. Yogi does meditation, Mulla does prayers, Pandit explains books and Siddh goes to Godly place ie remote hilly areas. His name has been explained in Shabad (Words) which only a few understand. Nanak, describes Him to be the one who resides everywhere ie water, earth and the sky'.

Guru Nanak's explaination that 'God is undescribable, God is without worries, God is the door to everything; every one has to leave this world, He only will stay', pleased Daulat Khan.

After staying for a few days with his sister and family at Sultanpur he took his family to Kartarpur Sahib.

Dr. S. S. Kohli gives an alternate route by which Guru Nanak reached East Punjab and not through West Punjab as stated. According to him, after Ladakh through, Daras, Balatal and Banderpur he is stated to have reached Hermukh Ganga on the Baramula side of the Jhelum where he sat under a chinar tree, the place held sacred in his memory. From Baramula the route adopted to Amarnath by the Guru is through Srinagar, Mattan, Bij-behera. He is stated to have returned to Mattan from Amarnath wherefrom, he went into Pir Panjal ranges and via Banihal, Kishtwar, Bhadarwah and Thathari, he reached Vaishno Devi. From Vaishno Devi, Guru Nanak visited Pur Mandal a distance of 15 miles from Jammu, Here the Guru is stated to have obtained the release of soul of the queen by touching a she jackal by his foot. He stayed near a mythical Jambavati cave where the king of Jammu came to him bare feet with valuable presents. His next stops are stated to be at Sujanpur, Pathankot and Gurdaspur before he reached Kartarpur. It is unlikely that Guru Nanak adopted this route, though his visit to Amarnath cave would have been completed before reaching Pehalgam from Leh as Amarnath is close to Balatal.

The route through West Punjab however, seems more logical as that was the general route adopted by travellers and sanyasis to Kashmir and back and Guru Nanak is stated to have travelled along well known tracks/ trails on which important religious centres/towns of political importance were situated.

References

1. Alexander Cunningham : *Attock District Gazetteer,* 1992, P.319.
2. Sarup Dass Bhalla : *Mahima Prakash.*
3. *Janam Sakhi Bhai Bala* : P.192.
4. *Janam Sakhi Bhai Mani Singh,* P.371.
5. Balwant Singh Anad : *Guru Nanak* P.187.
6. *Ain-e-Akbari* : Translated in English by Yadu Nath Sarkar Vol.II.
7. *Janam Sakhi Sodhi Meharban,* Calcutta, Vol.II, P.174.
8. Kahn Singh Nabha, *Mahan Kosh;* Language Department Punjab Patiala, P.785.
9. *Chahar-Bag-I-Punjab* : Genesh Das; Ed; Kirpal Singh, Khalsa College Amritsar, P.163.
10. Op Cit P, 223-4.
11. *Janam Sakhi Bhai Mani Singh* (Ed) Kirpal Singh (Dr), P.367.
12. *Walait Wali Janam Sakhi* (Ed). Kirpal Singh (Dr), P-35.
13. Surinder Singh Kohli, P.129-131.

Appendix 'A'

Expounder of Sikh Hymns of Guru Nanak. Ringdzin Rimpoche : An Interview

Chhimed Rigdzin Rimpoche, a 68 year old lama, is considered as the only lineage holder and reincarnation of Nunden Dorje (Undeposed Powerful Thunderbolt), the foremost disciple of Budh Sakyamuni. He is also recognised as the incarnation of Kyo-Chung Ltasa's Body, Nanam Dorje Dudjom's Speech and Guru Padmasambhava's Mind. He was made incharge of the 12 Gomphas (Monastries) in the Eastern Tibet at the age of 4 and have been controlling these even in 1958. After having migrated to India in 1958, he helped to establish the Tibetan Government in exile and refugee children' village and a handicraft centre. He recently retired after 25 years as the head on the Indo-Tibetan Studies Department of Shantiniketan University in West Bengal and is Lama of high standing within the Nyingma School of Tibetan Tantric Budhism. He is also an accomplished Yogi and has taught many religious students in Europe and America. His interest in Guru Nanak and in his scriptures is very deep and thorough as he considers Guru Nanak as one of the Guru Rimpoche of Nyingma sect. He has translated Japuji in Tibetan in consultation with the renowned scholar Rahul Sankratyan and is now on a visit to China and Tibet to deliver sermons and has agreed to trace out the route of Guru Nanak's travels in China and Tibet. I interviewed him during his recent visit to North Bengal University where his son U.C. Lama (a friend of mine) is a professor in the University. The extracts of the interview are produced :-

DSG : Would you tell me something about your life?

CRR : Though my name is Chimmed Ringdzen Rmpoche, but my more common name is CR Lama. I was born in East Tibet in 1922

(DSG : DS Grewal, CRR : Chhimed Rigdzin Rmpoche, UCL : UC Lama)

and recognised as reincarnation in 1925 when I was just 4 years old. I was born poor and my parents never expected that I will ever be honoured with such a great honour. During my recognition when Guru Rimpoche Sulthun Sumbhu, head of the local monastry indicated my being the reincarnation of Ninden Dorje, number of other children of my age belonging to richer families were brought before the counsel for consideration as reincarnation as the rich and the authorities did not want that I, son of a poor man, should be declared as the reincarnation of such an exalted Rimpoche. About 200 Lamas tested our virtues and recommended me. Finally 5 Head Lamas each from central and eastern Tibet tested me and found me to be the true re-incarnation. I was first recogninsed by the Realised Master Tulku Tsurlo and later by nine other lamas which included the Thirteenth Dalai Lama. Three very special Tang-rils (divinations) were performed in which various names were written on paper and placed inside dough balls. At each of these Tang-rils the only namewhich remained to floating in the water bowl was my name. These Tang-rils were performed in three highly auspicious places to guarantee their complete efficacy in front of Jowo Statue (the most ancient statue in Tibet) in the Jor-Khang temple in Lhasa and before the assembly of Lamas engaged in powerful Protector Rites at the Khordong Gompha (place of meditation). Finally I was declared as reincarnation and exalted Nunden Dorje.

DSG : Do you believe in reincarnation?

CCR : Don't you believe in 84 lakh jonies?

DSG : Do you still believe in miracles?

CDR : Yes. I will ask you to listen to a chapter from my own life. At the age of 9, I took a stone in my right hand and squeezed it thereby altering its shape. I being naughty as a child, used to be locked inside my room but due to my magical abilities, was always able to escape without breaking the door or lock. At the age of 10, I discovered two important volumes of Terma and an iron Terma box.

DSG : We Sikhs don't believe in miracles.

CRR : But Guru Nanak has shown number of miracles. He stopped a falling boulder in Punjab; he rotated Mecca; he also directed a poorman to the treasure in the lake in Bhutan. In Tibet he subdued demons with miracles, in Kokonoor he found treasures from lake.

DSG : Did Guru Nanak visit Tibet?

CRR : Yes. He did. He went to Mansarovar, he went to Lhasa; he went to Kokonoor lake, he visited Samya and Sakya monastries.

DSG : How can you say this?

CRR : We worship Nanak Lama in all our monastries and have installed his statues. We mention him in our prayers, we have mention of Guru Nanak in our books. I have also translated Japuji in Tibetan.

DSG : What all routes did he adopt while visiting Tibet?

CRR : The route I can't tell you exactly. But what I heard is that Guru Nanak or Nanak Lama or Guru Rimpoche as we call him, came from Rawalsar through Durang in Himachal Pradesh and visited Mansarovar and Kailash where he held discussions and created a greeat impression on local people and the saints. From Mansarovar he went to India probably and through Nepal crossed again to Tibet. He has visited Sakya Monastry and other adjoining areas. To my mind, he came to Sikkim from Sakya Monastry and went to Bhutan and to Lhasa through Tawang. Hand written scripts of Guru Nanak is stated to be preserved in Lhasa. He also visited Kokonoor lake, a sacred lake now in inner Mangolia. In Tibet he is known as Nanak lama, Guru Rimpoche and also Guru Guopka Maharaj. He visited Samya Monastry also probably on return from Tibet. Enroute he is stated to have visited Gokakula, a peak where even the vultures cannot reach.

DSG : Do the people in Tibet know about his visit?

CRR : Yes, I keep on visiting China and Tibet. There they mention about it.

DSG : Do you mean that he visited China also?

CRR : Yes. That is what I heard but I cannot say definitely. Guru Rimpoche had great powers.

DSG : When did you translate Japuji in Tibean?

CRR : I translated it in 1956-57 with the help of Rahul Sankratyan.

DSG : Did you get it published?

CRR : Not yet. I am eager to publish it but presently the manuscript is left at Shantiniketan where I tought for sometimes as Head of Tibetan Department.

DSG : I will be eager to get it published. Will you be able to get it by May-Jun?

CRR : I will try. Presently I am to go to Germany and then to China and Tibet On return, I will give it to you.

DSG : Thanks, Tashi Dille

CRR : Welcome again. Sat Sri Akal.

Appendix 'B'

2. Extract of An Interview with Shri J. K. Bhutia, Intelligence Officer, Thanggu

Place : Thanggu : Time: Nov.-Dec. 1987

DSG : Will you please tell me as to what all places in Sikkim did Guru Nanak Rimpoche go?

JKB : He came to Sikkim from Tibet via Nakula and visitied Gnalung where he rested. The area was very foggy and soggy and looked as if it is like hell hence Guru Nanak called it hell because Gnalung in Tibetan means 'valley of hell'. Guru Nanak's hand marks can be seen on a boulder in Gnalung.

Therefrom, he visited the Muguthang valley. There a Rakshash (demon) known as Rambha used to reside in the valley. He was harrassing the human beings and the cattle. Guru Nanak found him to be destructive and powerful and considered bringing him to True Path. The demon came to know about Guru Nanak's intention and also his powers. He changed his shape to various forms but could not escape from Guru Nanak's view. He became a tiger, an eagle, a fish and a rat turn by turn but Guru Nanak followed him throughout. Seeing this, he hid under a huge boulder thinking that he was out of the reach of Guru Nanak. Guru Nanak waited close to the boulder and started playing with two big boulders as do the children play with small pebbles. Rambha saw this from the hole he was hiding in. He came out to look at the play closely. Seeing this, Guru Nanak took out the weapon which, in Tibetan we call Phurba and threw at the demon. This destroyed the right eye of the demon. Rambha fell on Guru Nanak's feet. Guru Nanak advised him not to trouble human beings. Ramba took an oath never to trouble any human being or animal thereafter. He requested the Guru for the third eye which Guru granted him. Redeeming him, he proceeded further. From Muguthang he reached

Thanggu area via Lungnakla and stopped at the Choptha bridge. You might have seen a chorten close to the bridge where a small rivulet flows in the form of a snake. From Thanggu, Guru Rimpoche went to Chungthang and had his lunch. He went to Chungthang via Lachen. I also have the information from the local people and the Thanggu Lama who has most of the details. At Muguthang, Guru Nanak threw rice at the place close to where he was sitting. In Sikkim initially, we have had rice at that place only and no where else in the entire Lachen and Lachung valleys.

From Muguthang ,Guru Nanak proceeded to Lachung. In the area of Bichhu there used to be a very dangerous demon. This evil spirit was more powerful than that at Muguthang. In order to redeem this evil spirit, Guru Nanak followed him upto the jungles and caught it. He took out the tongue of this evil spirit and ordered it to worship the True Lord by keeping quiet.

Guru Nanak also visited Guru Dongmar. The people had a problem regarding water as all the lakes used to get frozen and poeple had no water to drink. They projected their problem to the Guru who hit the water of the lake with a stick.The place where he hit the lake never freezes. The water is also blessed by the Guru. The women who do not have children take it and are blessed with a child. Now a fair is organised every year by the local people on the lake area in honour of Guru Nanak's visit.

Appendix 'C'

3. An Interview with Head Lama of Lachen

Place : Lachen

Time : July 1988

DSG : Whom do you worship in this Gompha?

Head Lama : We worship Guru Rimpoche, whom you people call by the name of Guru Nanak.

DSG : Did Guru Nanak come to this place (Lachen)?

Head Lama : I am not very good at Hindi so I cannot explain you well. I can explain only in Tibetan.

DSG : In that case we will request this young friend to explain us in Hindi whatever you say in Tibetan.
(Through the interpretor).

DSG : Has Guru Nanak come to this place?

Head Lama : Guru Nanak visited this and other places in Sikkim of which the records are available in the Books. Guru Nanak went around in Sikkim when he came from Tibet. There is a country known as Chaol (Koel) in Tibet. The King of this country never worshipped God. That king put Guru Nanak in jail. Guru Nanak came out of jail automatically. There after he put him in fire. Guru Nanak came out unscathed. Again he put him in water. Guru Nanak did not drown. This surprised the king and he fell at the feet of the Guru. The king presented costly robes to the Guru. These clothes are preserved in this monasry and in the idol of this monastry you will find him wearing all these. The blue gown shown in this idol is the one offered by the king. This we have preserved in lock and key and take out only on particular days. (Note :- I saw the main idol which was about 15 feet high, of a saint in meditation. It was told to me to be belonging to Guru Nanak which is the chief idol in the Gompha and whom they worship. There was another idol of smaller size about 6 feet again told to be of Guru Nanak. Other idols were of Lord Buddha and one of the goddess Tara. There were two robes worn on Guru Nanak's idol; one red and another blue. The red was the one which according to them was given by the Lord-Himself while the blue was given by the king of Chaol in Tibet. The robe was well preserved in a glass case. He also showed me Guru Nanak's footprints on a stone).

DSG : Where did you get these foot marks from?

Head Lama : These foot prints were originally on a stone near Thanggu. We used to worship these and a fair used to be held. These were blown off during road construction. We found these with great difficulty from the Teesta river. This protion was lying unscathed. We brought it here with full reverence and installed in the Gompha.

DSG : Did he visit other places in Sikkim?

Head Lama : Yes, he visited numerous places in Sikkim and stayed here for about 85 days according to our records. The book is not at present here but is available at my home which I will bring and show it to you tomorrow. This book has complete records of Guru Nanak's life and his visit to Sikkim specially.

DSG : Can you tell me the name of other places where Guru Nanak visited?

Head Lama : There is a Hot Spring near Jaure Bridge about six kilometers from here. These hot springs are the creations of Guru Nanak. He has visited Chungthang as well Phodong ahead of Mangan. There are no marks available here but his hand marks are available in Thanggu. These are in between Kalep and Thanggu. His handmarks are on a big boulder. Guru Nanak visited Thanggu from Tibet and stayed there for some days. He crossed to Yumthang from Sabula probably. From Chungthang he visited Yoksom where Tibetan Army (Chinese Army) is camping at present. He visited about 100 places in Sikkim. He visited Muguthang. There is a place called Cheedand (Kidang) about 6 km north of Muguthang. Where there is again a handmark of Guru Nanak on a boulder. He visited Gurudongmar from Tibet and rested at Gurudongmar. He came to Thanggu from Gurudongmar. He went to Thanggu and then to Sabula, Yumthang and Lachung. Guru Nanak's handmarks are also preserved at Munsithang near the hot spring which again was found out by Guru Nanak. Complete history is in our book which I will read out to you. He has visited Sakya and Samya monastries in Tibet. He married a Tibet princess also. Details of this marriage is given on the wall paintings in the Lachung Monastry. Other details will be given to you tomorrow evening when we meet.

DSG : Tashi Dille.

Head Lama : Tashi Dille.

Note : This researcher went to contact Lama next day, but the Lama was evacuated to Gangtok, having fallen sick suddenly. He could not be contacted later. The painting of Guru Nanak were stated to be on the walls of Lachung Monastry about which Mrs Bali wife of Major Bali wrote an article in detail. However, on checking at Lachung, it was found that these paintings having gone old were colour washed and did not exist. According to the Lama, Lachung and Lachen there is a legend depicting Guru Nanak's Marriage with a Tibetan Princess, but which did not stand to further inquiry.

Appendix 'D'

4. Discussion with Lumpung Lama - Zimithang, Arunachal Pradesh

Place : Lumpung (Arunachal) Time : Oct. 1989

The Lumpung monastry connected with Tawang by mountainous foot tracks is situated on the slopes to Zimithang Valley, This valley located on the route from Tawang to Tibet is very close to Arunachal - Tibet border. Therefrom foot tracks lead to Lhasa the state capital of Tibet, and to Samya Monastry, the most prominent monastry of Western Tibet. Reaching there in an Air Force helicopter in Oct. 1989, I held discussions with the Lama of Lumpung at Lumpung monastry in connection with Guru Nanak's visit to that part of Arunachal Pradesh and Tibet. Information gathered is given in the form of an interview.

Q. Since what time are you here?

Ans. I was born and brought up here. My forefathers too lived in this place after they migrated from Tibet.

Q. When did they migrate to this place?

Ans. About 500 years ago there was a war between GelugPa and Nyingma - Pa sects in which GelugPa sect won and we were put through number of miseries. Finally our people had to leave Central Tibet and we settled here. At that time there used to be no clear boundaries between India and Tibet. We came to know of it after 1962 only.

Q. What is your sect?

Ans. I am from NyingaMa - Pa sect. We follow Mahayana Budhism. We also follow Nanak Lama. His 10 feet idol is one of the Chief decties in this Gompha and we worship it.

Q. When and how did your sect establish faith in Guru Nanak

Ans. When we were being ousted from our area, Nanak Lama came to solace us and to show sympathy. He blessed us with prosperity and freedom. That is why we are more prosperous and free than those in Tibet. Before this war, the king of Tibet was a NyingMaPa who had listened to Nanak Lama's discourses and became his follower. Our complete sect followed the king and we started having the idol of Nanak Lama in our Gomphas. When Nanak Lama visited this place, we were in a quite desperate condition. With his blessings, we had good days.

Q. When and how did he visit this place?

Ans. He came here before Losar (The Tibetan New year which falls around January every year) from Tawang through Tashi Gompha and Zimithang and after some days' stay at this location, he proceeded to Lhasa.

Q. Can you show the idol?

Ans. Yes, it is inside the Gompha on the main pedestel (Lama Showed me an Idol of a size around 10 feet by 5 feet placed on the main platform. which I Photographed, The idol was not much different from other idols).

Q. It does not seem to be of Nanak Lama?

Ans. It is, as we felt it should be. It is not very old. We have not seen Nanak Lama. My grand father had got it made. It may not be the exact replica but this is how we visualise, Nanak Lama.

Appendix 'E'

An Interview with Capt. (Now Lt Col) Bikkar Singh (BS)

Place Siliguri Period Nov. 1989

DSG : Capt. Bikkar Singh, since how much time have you been in Bhutan?

BS : I am posted in Indian Military Training Team, Hawe, Bhutan and have been here for 2 years.

DSG : During your stay, did you find any evidence of Guru Nanaks' Travels to Bhutan?

BS : Yes, it is generally known among all local people that Guru Nanak has been in Bhutan. I have been in most of the cities of Western Bhutan and met various people. The people call Guru Nanak as Nanak Lama or Guru Rimpoche.

DSG : What all places he is stated to have visited in Bhutan? Also can you state the route he would have adopted through Bhutan?

BS : He came to Bhutan probably from Lhasa-Tibet side. He entered Bhutan from Phari-dzong in Tibet. From Pharidzong there are two routes to Bhutan which have been in use by various caravans. One route is via Rinchepotoe, Tremola, Somava, Chekha, Pavocha, Gunichara, Dukhey dzong and the other along Traomochu i.e. Dolang, Leng Matang, Yatung, Chumbi, Piptong, Choma, Cheni Gompha, Hugling, Asam Urukha, Tanzule, Khem Chekha, Sarithang, Kyula (13907), Hala, Damthang, Haw-Dzong, Chalvala, Paro. Accoording to evidence available he is stated to have adopted second route.

DSG : Have you got any written records available?

BS : No, not with me. In a room near my office, there are huge Volumes of Tibetan Manuscripts. Probably, they might be containing some information. I did not try so far, to interpret these due to lack of knowledge of the language.

Appendix 'F'

Interview with Lt Col Harpal Singh Bakshi

Place : Nashik   Date : 22 Oct. 93

Q. 1 How much time have you spent in Jammu & Kashmir?

Ans. I have spent three and a half years in Jammu & Kashmir as a pilot and have visited Ladakh area a number of times during this period.

Q. 2 When and from what route Guru Nanak visited Ladhakh? Can you describe the entire route or possible route?

Ans. Guru Nanak visited Leh Ladakh while returning from Mt Sumer and on his way to Kashmir Valley via Kargil in Ladakh. He adopted the route from Leh to Nimmu, Fatula, Kargil, Dras (Zozila), Baltal and to Amarnath.

Q. 3 What all places in Ladakh and Kashmir have been visited by Guru Nanak?

Ans. In Ladakh two prominent places came to my notice and these are being visited till today by most Sikh and non Sikh persons of Army. A Gurudwara has been constructed at a place Nimmu Road by Army units located near the area. Secondly, a very old tree in Leh proper is still existing where as per local people once Guru Nanak had halted. I am not aware of any place in Kashmir visited by Guru Nanak.

Q. 4 Can you give some background of Guru Nanak's visit to these places?

Ans. As mentioned earlier a Gurudwara now known as 'Pathar Sahib' exists on Leh Nimmu Road. As the legend has it, local people of Leh requested Guru Nanak that a Rakshas killed the passers by very frequently on the Leh--Nimmu tract and the people were terrorised and scared. Guru Nanak decided to camp in the said area. While he was meditating the Rakshas appeared on top of a rock and rolled a huge boulder from top of the hill with the intention of killing Guru Nanak.

Guru Nanak did not budge from his place of meditation and the boulder came and hit straight into the back of Guru Nanak. The Rakhshas came down the hill with the intention of appreciating his kill and converting it as his meal. He was however shocked in disbelief to find that the boulder had melted and a big cavity had been formed in its end while no damage had been done to the Guru. The Demon, upon realising that he had confronted a God's man, fell on the feet of Guru Nanak and was thus. redeemed.

Q. 5 Have you some photographs of the area?

Ans. Yes, I produce three photographs of Gurudwara Patthar Sahib and the adjoining hill.

Bibliography

English

1. Ahuja, N. D. : *Great Guru Nanak and Muslims,* Chandigarh, Kirti Publishing House, 1974, XVI, 214 P.
2. Anand, Balwant Singh : *Guru Nanak,* New Delhi, Guru Nanak Foundation, 1983, 223 P.
3. Ardaman Singh Bhayee :*One Guru, One Movement,* Patiala, Guru Nanak Mission.
4. Bal, Sarjit Singh :*Life of Guru Nanak,* Chandigarh, Punjab University, 1970, VIII, 285 P.
5. Benerjee Anil Chandra : *Guru Nanak and His Times,* Patiala Punjabi University, 1971, 245 p.
6. ———— : *Guru Nanak to Guru Gobind Singh,* Allahabad, Rajesh Pub. 1978, 244 P.
7. Benerjee, Indu Bhushan : *Evolution of the Khalsa,* Vol I, *Foundations of the Sikh Panth,* University of Calcutta, 1936.
8. Banerjee, S. K. : *Humayun Patshah, 1508-40,* Calcutta, 1938.
9. Bedi, P. L. : *Guru Baba Nanak,* New Delhi, New Light Pub. 1971, 136 p.
10. ———— : *Prophet of the Full Moon : Guru Baba Nanak The Founder Master of Sikhism,* New Delhi, New Light Pub. 1976, 288p.
11. Bele Charles : *Tibet, Past and Present,* Oxford, 1929.
12. Beveridge, A. S. : *The Babur Nama, in English, 2 Vols,* London, 1921.
13. Bhagat Singh : *Guru Nanak of Talwandi,* Amritsar, Sikh Pub. House.
14. Bhikshu Sangharista : *A Survey of Buddhism*
15. Bija Roy Burman : *Religion and Politics in Tibet,* New Delhi, Vikas Publishing House.
16. Bingley, A. H. : *The Sikhs,* Simla, 1899, Reprint 1990, Delhi.
17. Briggs, G. W. : *Gorakhnath and Kampatta Yogis, 1933.*
18. Briggs John (Jr) : *History of the Rise of the Mohammadan Power in India till the year AD 1612.*

19. Chawla Harbans Singh (ed) : *Guru Nanak : The Prophet of the people,* New Delhi, Gurudwara Shri Guru Singh Sabha, 1970, XVI, 104+130+69P.
20. Chopra, P.N. : *Some Aspects of Social life During the Mughal Age (1526-1707),* Agra, 1943.
21. Bawa, Chhaju Singh : *The Ten Gurus and Their Teachings,* Lahore, 1903.
22. Cunnigham, Joseph Davey : *A History of the Sikhs from the origination of the Nation to the Battle of the Sutlej,* London, John Murray, 1849, 1851, 1853, O.U.P., 1918.
23. ———— : *Life of Baba Nanak, the Founder of Sikh Sect,* Indian Anitquiry, iii, 1874.
24. Cust, Robert Needham : *Linguistic and Oriental Essays.* Vol. 3, The Indian Performer - Guru Nanak (511-520), London, Trubener & Co, 1804-1903.
25. Dalip Singh (J. Auth) : *Guru Nanak Dev and His Teachings,* Jalandhar, Raj Pub. 1969, 418 p.
26. Daljit Singh, Raja; Sir : *Guru Nanak,* Lahore, 1943 (R) Ludhiana, Guru Nanak Mission Society. 1971, 257 P.
27. Daljit Singh (J. Auth) : *Great Humanist, Guru Nanak,* Language Department, Punabi University, 1970, 160 P.
28. Fauja Singh and Arora, A.C. (Eds) : *Papers on Guru Nanak,* Proceedings of the Punjab History Conference, 4th Session, 1969, Patiala, Punjabi University, 1970, 240 P.
29. Fauja Singh and Kirpal Singh (Drs.) : *Atlas : Travels of Guru Nanak,* Patiala, Punjabi University, 1976.
30. Field Dorothy : *The Religion of the Sikhs,* London, 1914.
31. Francis, Eric : *Guru Nanak* : Bombay, Purohit and Sons, 1970, 120p.
32. Gait, Edward : *A History of Assam,* Calcutta, Supdt. Govt. Plg India, 1926, 383 P.
33. Ganda Singh : *Guru Nanak : His Life and Teachings,* Singapore Sikh Missionary Trust Society, Singapore, 1940.
34. ———— : *Sources of Material on the life and Teachings of Guru Nanak (The Punjab, Past and Present,* Vol III, 1969), Patiala Deptt of Punjab Historical Studies, Punjabi University, 1969, 444 P.

35. Gill, Pritam Singh : *Doctring of Guru Nanak,* Jullunder, New Book Co., 1969, 182 P.
36. Gopal Singh : *Guru Nanak,* New Delhi, National Book Trust.
37. Gordon John, J. H. : *The Sikhs,* London, 1904
38. Gobind Singh Mansukhani (Dr.) : *Guru Nanak, World Teahcer.* New Delhi, IBH, 1968.
39. Grewal J. S. : *Guru Nanak in History,* Chandigarh, Punjab University, 1969 (R 1979). 348 P.
40. ———— : *Guru Nanak to Maharaja Ranjit Singh,* Essays in Sikh History, Amritsar, Guru Nanak Dev University, 1972, 195 P.
41. Gupta, Hari Ram : *Life Sketch of Guru Nanak,* Delhi, National Pub. House, 1968, 32 P.
42. Gurbaksh Singh : *Sikh Relics in East Bengal, Decca Review,* 1915, 196 PPP 1-1, 72-93.
43. Gurmukh Nihal Singh : *Guru Nanak - His Life, Time and Teachings,* Delhi, National Pub. House, 1969, 305P.
44. Haig, J. Wolseley (Jr) : *Muntakhubut Tawrikh,* Bibliotheca Indica Series, Calcutta, 1899.
45. Harbans Singh : *Guru Nanak*, Patiala, Punjabi Univ, 1969, 62P.
46. *Guru Nanak and the Origins of the Sikh Panth*, Bombay, Asia Pub. House, 1969, 247p.
47. Harbans Singh (ed) : *Perspectives on Guru Nanak : Seminar Papers,* Patiaia, Punjabi Univ, 1975 xii, 549P.
48. Harnam Dass : *Guru Nanak's Philosophy of Divine Life,* Chandigarh, Juneja Pub, 1969, xii, 150p.
49. India, Ministry of Information and Broadcasting, Publication Division : *Guru Nanak,* New Delhi, 1969, xvii, 224p.
50. Ishar Singh : *Nanakism : A New World Order, Temporal and Spiritual* , New Delhi, Ranjit Pub. House, 1967, xv, 288p.
51. _______ *Philosophy of Guru Nanak - A Comparative Study,* New Delhi, Ranjit Pub. House, 1969, 274P.
52. Jodh Singh : *Gospel of Guru Nanak in His own Words,* Patiala, Language Dept., Punjab, 1969, viii, 197P.
53. ______ : *Guru Nanak Lectures,* Madres Univ., 1969, 64P.
54. ______ : *Teachings of Guru Nanak,* Delhi, National Pub. House, 1969, 26p.

55. Jogendra Singh (Comp) : *Thus Spoke Guru Nanak - A Collection of the sayings of Guru Nanak,* 2nd ed, Chandigarh, Punjab Religious Society, 1967, viii, 113p.

56. Joginder Singh Sahi : *Sikh Shrines in India & Abroad,* Faridabad, Common World, 1978.

57. Jogindra Singh and Daljit Singh : *Great Humanist : Guru Nanak,* Patiala, Languages Department, 1970, 160p.

58. Johar, Surinder Singh : *Guru Nanak,* Jullunder, New Book Co., 1969, 178p.

59. _____ *Guru Nanak : A Biography,* Jullundur New Book Co., 1969 259p.

60. Kartar Singh : *Guru Nanak Dev : Life & Teachings,* Ludhiana, Lahore Book Shop, 1969, vii, 352p.

61. Khushdeva Singh : *At the Feet of Guru Nanak,* Patiala Guru Nanak Foundation Committee, 1969, 41p.

62. Khushwant Singh, (Tr) : *Hymns of Guru Nanak,* New Delhi, Orient Longmans, 1969 xv, 207P (UNESCO Collection, of Representative Works - Indian series.

63. Kohli Surinder Singh : *Philosophy of Guru Nanak,* Chandigarh, Punjab Univ 1970 vii 200P.

64. _____ :*Travels of Guru Nanak,* Chandigarh, Punjab Univ., 1970, vii, 200p.

65. Lalvani K.T., *Beyond No Ones Reach,* London, Guru Nanak Foundation, 1969, 56p.

66. Manfred Gerner and Ahluwalia H.P.S. (Maj) : *Himalaya, New Delhi,* Himalayan Books, 1985.

67. Manmohan Singh : *Life of Shri Guru Nanak Japji and Asa Di Var,* Dehra Dun, Jiwan Singh, 1972, 105+58p.

68. Manmohan Singh (tr) : *Hymns of Guru Nanak,* Patiala, Punjabi Univ., 1972, xiv, 954p.

69. Mansukhani, Gobind Singh : *Guru Nanak, The Apostle of Love,* New Delhi, Hemkunt Press, 1970, 120p.

70. _____ : *Guru Nanak : World Teacher,* New Delhi, India Book House, 1968, vi, 96p.

71. _____ : *Life of Guru Nanak,* New Delhi, Guru Nanak Foundation, 1974, xii, 137p.

72. McLeod W.H. : *Guru Nanak and the Sikh Religion*, Bombay, Oxford Univ. Press, 1969, 49p.

73. Narang, Gokul Chand : *Glorious History of Sikhism (From the Times and the Teachings of Guru Nanak to the Death of Maharaja Ranjit Singh)*, 6th ed, New Delhi, New Book Society of India, 1972, 303p.

74. Punjab History Conference, 4th Session, Patiala, 1969 *Papers on Guru Nanak* (ed) by Fauja Singh and A.C., Arora, Patiala, Punjabi Univ., 1970, 240p.

75. Language Department Punjab, *Hymns of Guru Nanak*, Patiala, 1972, xxxvi 954p.

76. Raghavacar, SS & Ramakrishnarao, K.S. (eds) *Guru Nanak : His Life and Teachings*, Mysore, Mysore Univ., 1971, vi, 83p.

77. Ramakrishnarao, K.S. : *Guru Nanak, His Life and Teachings*, Mysore Univ 1971, vi, 83p.

78. Sekhon, Sant Singh : *Guru Nanak Today : An Anthology*, Jandiala, Guru Gobind Singh Republic College, 1970, Vi, 134p.

79. Shamsher Singh and Virdi, Narendra Singh : *Life of Guru Nanak, Through Pictures*, Amritsar, Modern Shitya Academy, 1969, 92p.

80. Shan, Harnam Singh (ed) : *Guru Nanak in His Own Words*, Amritsar, Chief Khalsa Diwan, 1970, xxiii, 120p.

81. Shanta, Sarbjeet Singh : *Nanak, The Guru*, New Delhi, Orient Longmans, 1970, 174p.

82. Sharma M.C. (tr) : *Story of Guru Nanak*, Patiala, Punjabi Univ, 1970, 38p.

83. Sohan Singh : *Guru Nanak : A Brief Biography*, Ludhiana, Lyall Book Depot, 1968, 132p.

84. Talib, Gurbachan Singh : *Guru Nanak : His Personality and Vision*, Delhi, Gurdas Kapur, 1969, xxxii, 327p.

85. _____ :*Guru Nanak*, New Delhi, Sahitya Academy, 1984.

86. Taran Singh. (ed) : *Guru Nanak and Indian Religious Thought*, Patiala, Punjabi Univ. 1970 243p.

87. Trilochan Singh : *Guru Nanak : Founder of Sikhism : A Biography*, Delhi, G.P.C., 1969, xi, 510P.

88. Vaswani, T.L. : *Guru Nanak*, Poona, Gita Pub House, 1970.

89. Virdi, Narendra Singh (Jt. Auth) : *Life of Guru Nanak Through Articles Pictures*, Amritsar, Modern Sahitya Academy 1969, 92P

90. Balwant Singh : *Guru Nanak's visit to Uch-Sharif,* (Bahawal pur State Now in Pak.) *Spokesman,* 18 (2), 6 Jan 1969 : 2.

91. Banerjee, Kali Charan : *"Meeting of Sri Guru Nanak Dev and Sri Natyananda Dev" : Sikh Review,* 22 (251) Nov. 1974, 49p.

92. Bharpur Singh : *Guru Nanak's Mission in Foreign Countries: Spokesman* 24 (12), Guru Nanak Number, 1974.

93. Chhabra, G.S. : *Guru Nanak's Travels : Spokeman" 18(11-12)* Guru Nanak Number 1968, 61-62.

94. Dawe, Donald G : *'Relevance of Guru Nanak's Philosophy in Modern Age', Spokesman 19(12-13),* Guru Nanak Quincentenary Number 1969, 147-148 : *Thought,* 21(48), 29 Nov 1969, *Sikh Review,* 18(202), Sept. 1970: 20-21.

95. Devinder Singh : *Guru Nanak and the Modern World, Sikh Review* 22(257) May 1975 : 18-20 *Spokesman* 26 (5) o4 Oct 1976: 3-4.

96. Dharam Paul : *"Guru Nanak - The Saviour, the Preacher", Spokesman,* 15(11-12) Guru Nanak Number 1965 : 43-44 & 46.

97. _____ : *'Guru Nanak and Religion Today' : Spokesman* 19(12-13), Guru Nanak Quincentenary Number, 1969, 99-106.

98. _____ : *'Heritage of Guru Nanak' : Spokesman* 18(11-12) Guru Nanak Number 1968 : p.56.

99. Dharam Paul : *'Pilgrimage to Gurdwara Ritha Sahib' : Spokesman* 25 (12-13) Guru Nanak Number 1975 : 48.

100. _____ : *'Raja Yoga of Guru Nanak' : Sikh Review,* 24 (272) Aug 1976 : 35-37.

101. _____ : *'Two Glimpses of Guru Nanak' : Spokesman* 21(10), Guru Nanak Number 1971 : 46.

102. Dhyan Singh : *'Dialectical Spiritualism of Guru Nanak' : Spokesman* 24 (12), Guru Nanak Number 1974, 60.

103. _____ : *'Nanak Jheera' : Spokesman,* 26(27), 2 Mar 1977, 3 & 6.

104. Dosanjh, S.J. : *'Punjab of Guru Nanak', Sikh Review,* 22 (250) Oct 1974, 4-6.

105. Fauja Singh : *'Guru Nanak in Historical Perspective', Sikh Review,* 18(195) Oct-Nov 1969, 54-62.

106. Ganda Singh : *'Guru Nanak - A Bibilography' : Punjab Past and Present,* 3(1-2) 1969 : 425-444.

107._____ : *Guru Nanak at Puri : How it came to be Written Sikh Review,* 28 (318) Jun 1980, 28-30.

108. Ganda Singh : *'Guru Nanak with Chaitanya at Puri' : Sikh Review,* 18(195) Oct_Nov 1969 : 58-61.

109._____ : *'Guru Nanak's Impact of History', Punjab Past and Present,* 3(1-2) 1969, (413-423)

110._____ : *'Indian Society as Guru Nanak Found it', 'Sikh Review* 26(299) Nov 1978 : 5-9.

111. Gandhi, Surjit Singh : *'Place of Guru Nanak in History', Sikh Review,* 24 (275) Nov 1976, 33-35.

112. Gopal Singh : *'Life and Teachings of Guru Nanak Dev', Spokesman,* Guru Nanak Number 26(9) : 1976 : 9.

113. Grewal, Dalvinder Singh, (Colonel. Dr.) : *'Guru Nanak in Menchukha', The Sikh Review,* Nov.1987.

114._____ : *'Guru's Travels Through Sikkim', The Sikh Review,* Vol xxxvi, No. 419,Nov. 1988, p.25-31.

115._____ : *The Amazing Trevels of Guru Nanak - Journey to Bhutan', The Sikh Review* Vol xxxvii : V No. 425, Jun 1989, p.30-31.

116._____ : *'Guru Nanak in Arunachal Pradesh' The Sikh Review.* Vol xxvii; VI, No. 426, June 1989, p.48-53.

117._____ : *The Amazing Travels of Guru Nanak-Journey Through Assam, The Sikh Review,* Vol xxxvii, VII, No. 428, Aug, 1989, p.37-42.

118._____ : *'Guru Nanak's Travels to Kashmir' The Sikh Review,* Nov 1989, P.24,32.

119._____ : *The Amazing Travels of Guru Nanak : Discourses with Yogis and Journey through Tibet, The Sikh Review,* Nov 1989, p.41-53

120._____ : *'Guru Nanak's Journey through Himachal Pradesh' : The Sikh Review,* Vol XXXVII, VIII, No. 440, Aug 1990, p.23-6.

121._____ : *'Guru Nanaks' Journey into Garhwal Kumaon Hills', The Sikh Review,* Vol XXXVIII. IX, No. 441, Sept, 1990, p.19-27.

122. Gurdeep Singh : *'Sultanpur Lodhi', Spokesman* 23 (12-13) Guru Nanak Number 1973, 41-42.

123._____ : *Travels of Guru Nanak, 'Spokesman,* 19 (12-13) Guru Nanak Quincentenar Number 1969 37-38 and 139.

124._____ : *'One of the most Widely Travelled Prophets',* Times of India, 22 Nov 1969, 14.

125. Gurmukh Nihal Singh : *'Janam Sakhis : Their Interpretation and Value' Spokesman,* 19 (12-13), Guru Nanak Quincentenary Number 1969 37-38 and 139.

126. Gurtej Singh : *'Guru Nanak' : Orissa Review,* 26(4) Nov 1969 : 5-7

127._____ : *'Guru Nanak and the Mediaeval Bhaktas', Sikh Review,* 21 (232), March 1972, 2-4.

128. Harbans Singh : *'Educational Philosophy of Guru Nanak': Spokesman* 21 (15), 6 Dec 1971 : 5:27 (2) 29 Aug 1977 : 5, *Sikh Review,* 29 (296), Aug 1978, 18-19.

129._____ : *'Guru Nanak at Kartarpur', Spokesman* 19 (12-13), *Guru Nanak Quincentenary Number* 1969, 59-62 : *Sikh Review,* 21 (240) Nov 1973 : 11-21.

130. Hari Singh and Meerjani, K : *'Guru Nanak at Bhadrak', Sikh Review,* 18(195) Oct-Nov 1969 : 62-64.

131. Harnam Dass : *'Educational Philosophy of Guru Nanak' Spokesman,* 21(15), 6 Dec 1971 : 5 27(2) 29 Aug 1977 :5, *Sikh Review,* 29 (296), Aug 1978 - 18-19.

132. Hazara Singh : *'Guru Nanak Dev' : Sikh Review,* 20 (228) Nov 1972 : 15-20.

133. Issar, N.S. : *'Guru Nanak's visit to Tibet' Punjab Past and Present* : 3(1-2), 1969, 329-333.

134. Jagdev Singh : *'Guru Nanak and Babar Invasion', Spokesman* 19(11) 3 Nov 1969 : 7

135._____ : *'Guru Nanak's Alignment with the World', Spokesman,* 29 (9), *Guru Nanak Number,* 1976 : 20.

136._____ : *'Travellers of the same Track : Sant Namdeo and Guru Nanak', Lok Rajya,* 26(13) Nov 1970, 5-9

137. Johar, Surinder Singh : *'Age of Guru Nanak' Spokesman,* 28(11-12) Guru Nanak Number 1978, 23-26.
138. Kalra, Balwant Singh : *'Guru Nanak's Visit to Uch Sharif', Sikh Review,* 18(188) March 1969 : 11-12.
139. Kalra, Mohan Singh : *'Guru Nanak's Mission to the Muslims', Punjab Past and Present,* 3(1-2) 1969, 299 311.
140. Kapur Singh : *'Guru Nanak' : Sikh Review,* 24(275), Nov 1976, 5-31.
141. Karunratna, Saddhamangala : *'Guru Nanak's Visit to Ceylon', : Sikh Review, 18,* (195) Oct Nov 1969 : 84-85.
142. Khan, Abdul Majid : *'Guru Nanak and Islam': Sikh Review,* 25 (287) No. 1977 : 19-23.
143. Kharag, Ranjit Singh : *'Date of Birth of Guru Nanak' : Spokesman* 18(11-12) *Guru Nanak Number* 1968 39-40.
144. Kirpal Singh : *'Did Guru Nanak go to Ceylon' ; Sikh Review,* 18 (195) Oct-Nov 1973, 79 : 5 : 8
145. _____ : *'Guru Nanak in Ladakh' Punjab Past and Present,* 3 (1-2): 1969, 325-326).
146. _____ : *'Message of Guru Nanak' Spokesman* 19 (12-13) *Guru Nanak Quincentenary Number* 1969 : 36 *Bihar Information* 17 (19), 16 Nov 1969 : 2
147. _____ : 'Miracle of Guru Nanak' Spokesman 15 (11-12) Guru Nanak Number, 1963 29.
148. Kohli, Surinder Singh : *'Cosmology As Propounded by Guru Nanak', Spokesman,* 29 (50) 11 Aug 1980 : 5
149. _____ : *'Guru Nanak in Arabia', Organiser,* 23 (16), 29 Nov 1969 : 11-12
150. _____ : *Guru Nanak in Uttrakhand 'Spokesman,* 24 (12) *Guru Nanak Number* 1974 : 39.
151. _____ : *'Legendary Journey of Guru Nanak', Spokesman,* 19(12-13) *Guru Nanak Number*
152. _____ : *'Sea Journeys of Guru Nanak' Spokesman* 23 (12-13) *Guru Nanak Number*
153. Kulraj Singh : *'Baba Goest East' : Sikh Review 18(195)* Oct-Nov 1969 : 47-57.

154. Ladha Singh : *'Guru Nanak and Rank of Kanya Kumari' Spokesman,* 18(11-12) *Guru Nanak Number:* 1968 : 55 : 19 (2), 25 Aug 1969 : 8.

155. _____ : *'Guru Nanak Reformed the Cannibals', Spokesman* 20 (12) *Guru Nanak's Visit to Eminabad, Spokesman*19 (8) 13 Oct

156. Majumdar RC : *'Guru Nanak's Impacton Indian History', Sikh Review,* 18 (195) Oct-Nov 1969 105-113.

157. Manjeet Singh : *'Guru Nanak Visit to Baghdad' : Sikh Review,* 18 (195) Oct_Nov 1969 : 120-127.

158. Mansukhani, Gobind Singh : *'Guru Nanak's Visit to Eastern India' Spokesman,* 19 (16) 15 Dec 1969: 6

159. McLeod, W.H. : *'Life of Guru Nanak according to Bhai Gurdas', 'Punjab Past and Present'.*

160._____ : *'Procedures in Analysing the Sources of life of Guru Nanak', Journel of Indian History,* 45(I), April 1967 : 207-27.

161. Mohan Singh : *'Baba Goes South' : Sikh Review* 18 (195) Oct-Nov 1969, 68-78.

162._____ : *Delving Deep into Guru Nanak Travels", Spokesman,* 15(11-12) Guru Nanak Number 1965, 55-56.

163. _____ : *'Kartarpur : Nursery of Sikhism', Sikh Review* 18(195) Oct-Nov 1969 : 96-102.

164. Nayyar, Gurbachan Singh : *'Guru Nanak and the Ultimate Reality', Spokesman,* 30 (12-13) *Guru Nanak Number* 1980 : 15-16.

165. _____ : *'Guru Nanak Dev in Historical Perspective', Spokesman,* 25 (12-13)

166._____ : *'Travels and Impact of Guru Nanak', Spokesman,* 29 (9-10) *Guru Nanak Number,* 1979 : 27-28.

167. Parkash Singh : *'Guru Nanak's Visit to Ceylon', Spokesman,* 21(10), Guru Nanak Number, 1971 35-37.

168. Parman Singh : *'Guru Nanak's Dialogues with Yogis', Sikh Review,* 22 (243), Feb-Mar 1974 5-8.

169. Partap Singh Shant : *'Amazing Travels of Guru Nanak', Sikh Review,* Vol.38 :11, No. 443, Nov.1990. P.27-8.

170. Peace M.L. : *'Bhai Mardana's Departure', Spokesman,* 14 (3) 22 Mar 1965.

171. Peace M.L. : *'Guru Nanak at Banaras', Spokesman,* 16 (19) 26 Dec 1966, 5-6.

172._____ : *'Guru Nanak as Historians Discovered Him', Spokesman* 14(27) 1st Mar. 1965, 5

173. Rajinder Singh : *'Guru Nanak as Historians Discovered Him', Spokesman,* 25 (12-13) Guru Nanak Number 1975 27 : 28.

174._____ : *'Relevance of Guru Nanak's Teachings Today' Spokesman,* 27 (13-14), Guru Nanak Number, 1977 : 19.

175. Ram Singh : *'Fearless Guru Nanak' Spokesman,* 25 (12-13) Guru Nanak Number 1975, 39-41

176. Rattan Kaur : *'Guru Nanak at Sultanpur', Spokesman* 16(I) Anniversary Number 1966, 63:64.

177. Santokh Singh : *'Great Exponent of Dharma' ; Sikh Review,* 22 (247) Jul 1974, 30 : 32.

178. _____ : *'Guru Nanak's Impact on the Siddha' Spokesman,* Guru Nanak Number 26 (9), 1976,30.

179. Sewa Ṛam Singh : *'Guru Nanak at Baghdad' : Punjab Past and Present,* 3 (1-2) 1969, 340 : 343

180. Srinivasa Ayyangar R : *'Guru Nanak after 500 years', Indian Literature,* 13 (2), Jun 1970, 30-36.

182. Surjit Singh : *'Glimpses From Guru Nanak's Life', Spokesman,* 19(9) 20 Oct 1969, 6

183. Surma, M.S. : *'Travels of Guru Nanak', Spokesman,* 18 (46), 21 Jul 1969, 14, 18 (47), 28 July 1969 6 & 10:19(2), 25 Aug 1969, 4:19 (3), 01 Sep 1969, 08:19 (5), 15 Sep 1969 : 7 : 19(6) 22 Sep 1969, 6 & 11 : 19 (7), 29 Sep 1969 : 6

184. Tak Raghubir Singh and Sagar Sabinderjit Singh : *'Guru Nanak's visit to Bhadrak' : Journal of Sikh Studies,* 4(1) Feb 1977 : 147 165.

185._____ : *'Guru Nanak's Visit To Dacca' : Journal of Sikh Studies* 4(2) Aug 1977 : 117-129

186._____ : *'Guru Nanak's Visit to Kharagpur, Midnapur and Chanderkona' : Journal of Sikh* Studies 2(1) Feb 1975 : 134-153.

187._____ : *'Guru Nanak's Visit to Jagnnath Puri', Journal of Sikh Studies,* 3(2) Aug 1976 158-175.

188. _____ : *'Guru Nanak's Visit to Maldah' : Journal of Sikh Studies*

6(1) Feb 1979 : 163-167.

189. _____ : *'Guru Nanak's visit to Sasàram' : Journal of Sikh Studies,* 5(1) Feb 1978 : 177-184.

190. Tara Singh (Mrs) : *'Strong Haji', Sikh Review,* 17 (182) Sep 1968, 52.

191. Trilochan Singh : *'Guru Nanak and His Age' : Indo-Asian Culture* 19 (1) Jan 1970, 24-29.

192. Tarlochan Singh : *'Guru Nanak on Roof of the World', Sikh Review,* 18 (195) Oct-Nov 1969 86 : 95.

193. Taluka, Tarungpa : *'Guru Nanak in Tibet' : Punjab Past and Present* 3 (1-2) 1969 : 327-328.

194. Tur, Mohan Singh : *'Guru Nanak and Pilgrimage' : Spokesman* 19 (11) 3 Nov 1969 : 6

195. Vaswani, T.L. : *'Gospel of Guru Nanak', Spokesman,* 26 (11) 22 Nov 1976, 3-4-29 (3-4) 28 Annual Number.

196. _____ : *'Guru Nanak and Sant Kabir' : Spokesman,* 21 (10), Guru Nanak Number 1971,-17-18.

PUNJABI

197. Ashok, Shamsher Singh (Ed). : *'Purtan Janamsakhi : Sri Guru Nanak Devji',* Amritsar, SGPC, 1969.

198. Gurdas Bhai : *Varan,* Amritsar, S.G.P.C.

199. Gian Singh Giani : *Sri Guru Panth Parksah,* Patiala, Bhasha Vibhag, Punjab, 1970.

200. _____ : *Twarikh Guru Khalsa Panth,* Patiala, Bhasha Vibhag, Punjab.

201. Kirpal Singh (Dr) : *Janamsakhi Prampra,* Patiala, Punjabi University, 1969

202. Kahn Singh Nabha : *Mahan Kosh,* Patiala, Language Deptt, Punjab.

203. Lal Singh Sangrur (Giani) : *Guru Khalsa Twarikh,* Ludhiana, Lahore Book Shop, 1955.

204. Piar Singh (ed) : *Janamsakhi Sri Guru Nanak Devji,* (B-40) Amritsar, Guru Nanak Dev University, 1974.

205. Rattan Mohan Singh : *Sidh Ghosat : Sarab Pakhi Adhayan,* Ludhiana, Lahore Book Shop, 1970.
206. Sahib Singh (Prof) : *Jeevan Birtant Guru Nanak Devji,* Amritsar, Singh Bros, 1984.
207. Tarilochan Singh (Dr) : *Jeevan Chartar : Guru Nanak Dev,* Delhi Sikh Gurudwara Board, 1970
208. Teja Singh (Sodhi) : *Vachitar Jeewan Shri Guru Nanak Devji,* Amritsar, Bhai Chatter Singh Jeewan Singh, 1972
209. Teja Singh, Ganda Singh : *Sikh Itihas,* Patiala, Punjab University, 1985
210. Veer Singh (Bhai) : *Shri Guru Nanak Chamtkar,* Amritsar, Khalsa Samachar, 1955

Janamsakhis

1. *Puratan Janamsakhi Walwait Wali.*
2. *Janamsakhi Bhai Bala*
3. *Janam Sakhi Sodhi Meharban.*
4. *Janam Sakhi Bhai Mani Singh*
5. B-40 *Janamsakhi Guru Nanak Devji.*

Hindi

1. Jaggi Rattan Singh (Dr), 1975 : *Guru Nanak Viakatitav, Kritatuv aur Chintan,* Patiala, Bhasha Vibhag, Punjab, 1975
2. Santokh Singh Bhai, 1972 : *Guru Nanak Prakash (Part I&II)* Patiala, Bhasha Vibhag, Punjab, 1972
3. _____ : *Sri Guru Pratap Suraj Granth (Bhag-1),* Patiala, Bhasha Vibhag, Punjab, 1972
4. Sukha Singh : *Guru Bilas,* Patiala, Bhasha Vibhag, Punjab, 1978

Periodicals

English

1. *Advance,* Chandigarh.
2. *Calcutta Review,* (Monthly) Calcutta.
3. *Contemporary Indian Literature* (Monthly) New Delhi.
4. *Hindustan Times,* (Daily), New Delhi.
5. *Illustrated Weekly of India,* (Weekly) Bombay.
6. *Journal of Historical Research,* Ranchi.
7. *Journal of Indian History* (Three times in year) Trivandrum.
8. *Journal of Sikh Studies* (Bi-annual), Amritsar.
9. *KHERA,* Bhai Veer Singh Sahitya Sadan, New Delhi.
10. *Link,* (Weekly) New Delhi.
11. *Organiser,* (Weekly) Delhi.
12. *Panjab, Past and Present,* (Bi-annual) Patiala
13. *Sikh Review,* (Monthly) Calcutta.
14. *Spokesman* (Weekly), New Delhi.
15. *Times of India,* (Daily) New Delhi.
16. *Tribune,* (Daily), Chandigarh.

Punjabi

1. *Gurmat Prakash,* SGPC, Amritsar.
2. *Jagriti,* Chandigarh.
3. *Khoj Patriaka,* Punjabi University, Patiala.
4. *Parakh* Punjabi, University Chandigarh.
5. *Nanak Parkash Patrika,* Punjabi University, Patiala.
6. *Punjabi Duniya,* Bhasha Vibhag, Punjab, Patiala.
7. *Sikh Review,* Calcutta
8. *Sach Khand Patrika,* Nanded.
9. *Sis Ganj,* DGPC, Delhi.
10. *Singh Sabha Patrika,* Amritsar.